The High Engagement Work Culture

# The High Engagement Work Culture

## Balancing **Me** and **We**

David Bowles
*Consultant, Author, Speaker on Morale and Engagement at Work*
*www.moraleatwork.com*

and

Cary Cooper
*Distinguished Professor of Organizational Psychology & Health,*
*Lancaster University, UK Chair of the Academy of Social Sciences*

First published 2012 by
PALGRAVE MACMILLAN

Palgrave Macmillan in the UK is an imprint of Macmillan Publishers Limited, registered in England, company number 785998, of Houndmills, Basingstoke, Hampshire RG21 6XS.

Palgrave Macmillan in the US is a division of St Martin's Press LLC, 175 Fifth Avenue, New York, NY 10010.

Palgrave Macmillan is the global academic imprint of the above companies and has companies and representatives throughout the world.

Palgrave® and Macmillan® are registered trademarks in the United States, the United Kingdom, Europe and other countries.

ISBN 978–0–230–30449–9

This book is printed on paper suitable for recycling and made from fully managed and sustained forest sources. Logging, pulping and manufacturing processes are expected to conform to the environmental regulations of the country of origin.

A catalogue record for this book is available from the British Library.

A catalog record for this book is available from the Library of Congress.

10   9   8   7   6   5   4   3   2   1
21   20   19   18   17   16   15   14   13   12

Printed and bound in Great Britain by
CPI Antony Rowe, Chippenham and Eastbourne

# Contents

# List of Charts

# Dedications and Acknowledgments

## David Bowles

This book is dedicated to the memory of my mother, Colleen Bowles, who passed away at the age of 96½ while it was being written. She was an extraordinary woman who had lived in England her whole life, including through two world wars, with all that entailed. She generously passed along, through her genes and interactions, so many things that made her children stronger. I would also like to make a special dedication to Dr. George W. Stuart, retired nuclear physicist and all-round intellectual, who also made his passing during the writing of the book. George made my consulting firm's abilities so much greater with his custom database software we named RCI/In*Sight; my clients can often hardly wait to see the powerful data it has mined from their morale and engagement surveys.

Many people helped with the creation of this book, in so many ways, and I am grateful to all. My wife Janice is first on the list, lovingly supplying everything, from the emotional support that all authors need, to valuable advice on content in her specialized area of psychology.

I am grateful to V. Frank Asaro for the many conversations we have had during the year about his brilliantly simple concept of "co-opetition", which forms part of this book, and other ideas that I floated for inclusion in the book. Also to Jochen Frey at BMW's press office in Munich, who patiently took my calls for three months as I attempted to gain an interview, and to Harald Krüger, who generously granted that interview and took such great interest in it! My friends at the local Starbucks were their usual supportive selves, especially Frank and Andrew, Sasha and Meredith. At Palgrave Macmillan, I want to thank Stephen Rutt so much for taking a chance on our ideas for an improved, high engagement culture in our organizations, along with Hannah Fox, who shepherded us through the process in such a friendly way. Palgrave Macmillan's copy editors in Chennai, India, did a great job, and I want to thank P. M. Bhuvana Raj (or "Raj" as I know him) and his team for all their painstaking help and support. Physicist Professor Sir John Enderby was kind enough to grant an interview and enlighten me on the view that physics takes on the financial services industry. (*Full disclosure*: his status as my brother-in-law made the interview much easier to obtain!) Graef "Bud" Crystal, a man with an extraordinary history as probably the best known executive compensation "guru" of a generation in the US, was so helpful; his encouragement and extensive writings pointed me in the right direction to uncover some of the more egregious forms of the executive compensation "arms race" that so exemplifies the pay imbalance in many (US) organizations. Bud had the courage to stand against some of these excesses. I also want to say that John Mackey, co-founder and co-CEO of Whole Foods Market, which is featured as a case study in this book, was a real inspiration for what we had to say. For many years, and long before it became obvious how out of balance things were in many of our organizations, Mackey had been on the "road less travelled", slowly building a world class organization that lives and breathes so much of what we talk about in these pages. His strong acceptance in even the most capitalist-worshiping environments such as *The Wall Street Journal*, and his blending of card-carrying libertarianism with a softer side he calls "conscious capitalism", shows us that these ideas can draw from and be accepted by all parts of the political spectrum, while offering a positive way forward for society as a whole. Mackey's work personifies an optimal balance between "me" and "we" in the organizational world. Thanks too to the distinguished team of David MacLeod, Professor Ed Lawler, Dr. David Zinger and Dr. Pius Baschera for agreeing to preview and recommend our book.

Finally, a word about my co-author, Cary Cooper. I met him at Southampton University when I walked into his social psychology class for the first time. That was in 1970, and he has been a treasure trove of support and enthusiasm for me and my career ever since, including inviting me to be his very first Ph.D. student at UMIST in 1973. Cary is an inspiration to all with whom he comes into contact. It is an honor to have known him for more than 40 years, a fact that brings up many feelings of gratitude. To have now written two books with Cary is simply great. Thank you dear friend!

## Cary Cooper

I have really enjoyed working on this book with David. He was my first Ph.D. student, and when he contacted me again after many years saying he would like to write a book together, I was really moved and honored. I have four children and two grandchildren, and I feel that David is one of my family. I would like to dedicate this book to all my children, including David, and to my two new grandchildren, Jai Lucas Cooper and Isabella May George.

# Introduction and Background

The 2008 collapse of Lehman Brothers and Bear Stearns in the United States set off a systemic panic that almost engulfed the world's financial system. Only as a result of major efforts within the US and the UK, along with worldwide cooperation, were we able to pull back from the brink. Recent data shows that the US Federal Reserve lent no less than *$3.3 trillion* to prop up the world's economy, including to the Bank of England. The amount of money "lent, spent or committed," was an incredible *$7.7 trillion*, according the influential financial firm Bloomberg, which points out that even that number might be an underestimate.[1] Even the "unsinkable" Goldman Sachs received far more (and went to the "Fed" much more frequently) than had been thought. In one week in September 2008, *12 of the 13 largest US banks were technically insolvent*, including Goldman itself. Thanks to the rapid and successful recovery efforts, most still do not grasp the fact that the US was facing a *financial meltdown of far greater proportions than the Great Depression*. This is not our opinion, but that of an expert on that earlier period, Ben S. Bernanke, Chairman of the US Federal Reserve, speaking to the official US government enquiry into the Crash.[2]

Even some economies that had "appeared" relatively strong before were brought to their knees. No one had noticed what shaky ground they had been on until the Crash, which exposed all they were doing to put off their day of reckoning and rendered it useless. Such was its power that countries like Ireland have had to nationalize their entire banking system. Much of the industrial world (large swaths of north and south America, most of Europe and parts of Asia) is only just beginning to recover from this event; and the developing world, harnessed as it is to the well-being and "trickle down" effects of larger economies, was equally or more affected.

How could this happen? Clearly, out-of-control capitalist urges unleashing some of the baser human instincts, combined with lax oversight mixed with failed social engineering, nearly ruined the world's interconnected economy.

What are the longer-term consequences of this, and what can we learn from it? Can any country afford to go through this every now and then, shooting itself in the foot and taking years to recover from this self-inflicted injury, while its competition moves ahead?

In this book we look at the Crash of 2008 and the subsequent Great Recession through a different prism than that of the numerous government reviews and press articles. While recognizing the part played by government, *we look instead at its genesis within our organizations and its effect on the most precious resource in any organization: its people.* We ask the questions we believe need to be asked: *most importantly, whether we can change our behavior within these organizations in such a way that it is far less likely to happen again.* Specifically, we look at:

- What happened before and during this Crash? What part of the Crash relates to how we manage our organizations, and to the "culture" within them?
- If this "work culture" is at least partly to blame, what elements within that culture can we identify that led to this catastrophic event? Did greed and "ego-centric" ("me" instead of "we") values act as a partial driver of behavior in some of the organizations involved in the Crash? If so, is this simply inevitable as a by-product of any human endeavor or is it part of a seriously dysfunctional element that needs to change? Is it widespread even outside the financial services industry?
- Has there been a backlash to what happened? Do emerging political trends such as the "Tea Party" and "Occupy Wall Street" in the US and elsewhere represent an attempt to redress some of the underlying and unwritten cultural "values" in our organizational life, which led to this Crash?
- What effect has the Crash of 2008 had on the morale and engagement of our workforce? Has there been damage in that area, or will there be in the future if we continue this way? Were worker engagement levels high, even before the Crash? If not, why not?
- Have those parts of the work culture that led to the Crash also damaged worker morale and engagement, even during the pre-Crash period?
- Can we emerge from the Great Recession not only with the desire to change but also with insights that allow us to build a *sustainable, high engagement work culture*, which (a) does not subject us to the periodic prospect of ruin because of the actions of a few, while (b) still maintaining the capitalist system that has brought such prosperity to the world?
- If so, how might this look, and is anyone successfully working this way now?

These questions are not just speculation; many countries, including the US, UK and those in continental Europe such as Germany, France and Italy, *do not enjoy high levels of worker morale and engagement*; in fact several are below average on a worldwide basis. This detracts significantly from organizational performance: morale and engagement are not only correlated with, *but drive key performance factors* such as productivity, profitability, customer satisfaction and worker health, as we demonstrated in detail in 2009.[3] Even before the Crash, therefore, many countries around the world were running at an "engagement deficit" in their workplaces.

By sustaining the culture that leads to this in many of their major organizations, they are missing the opportunity to manage people in a different way, creating much higher worker engagement, and generating the enormous performance benefits that flow from this.

We believe we indeed can "do things better" to create this high work engagement scenario, and draw on the parallel trends of sustainability in the environmental world and especially the movement from "me" to "we", which is already starting to be seen even in the very companies that were at the heart of the Crash, and in some societies at large. To add urgency to the theme for those most affected by the years of the financial meltdown, emerging giants such as China and India hardly slowed down at all during this period; this means that many Western and other countries that participated in this catastrophic event can hardly afford to repeat such self-destructive behavior in the future, if they wish to pass on their standard of living to the next generations.

# Part I
# What Has Happened to Our Work Culture and Why?

# 1

# The Crash of 2008: What Happened and Why Did It Happen?

As a scholar of the Great Depression, I honestly believe that September and October of 2008 *was the worst financial crisis in global history, including the Great Depression.*

Ben S. Bernanke, Chairman, US Federal Reserve, quoted in the US Financial Crisis Inquiry Commission (FCIC) report, published early in 2011 (emphasis added)[1]

## Causes of the Crash: Most frequently cited

We've survived; some would even say it's almost like it never happened. That we did is only testimony, however, to the skill of those who presided over these events at the head of governments in the US and Europe. Chairman Bernanke's quote above should give us pause. It was much worse than we might like to admit. Like a patient recovering from a serious, life-threatening operation, it is easy to forget afterwards how bad things were. Maybe we need some more help remembering so that we can be sure to do something this time? Mr. Bernanke can assist us again: as quoted in the FCIC Report,[2] he said that during the autumn of 2008, of the 13 most important US financial institutions, "*12 were at risk of failure within a period of a week or two*." That's right, it was a total meltdown, and only J. P. Morgan Chase would have survived without massive government intervention. The "Masters of the Universe" rescued by the US government? One would think that such a humbling experience would change behavior; but did it? Certainly, regulation has been tightened and governments everywhere have vowed to not let this happen again. Now, only time will tell.

By now, most people are aware of the witches brew of lax and poorly conceived government regulation, sloppy or nonexistent enforcement of rules and regulations and cheap money, which tempted everyone from ego-driven CEOs to brainy financial product engineers to legions of others (including less-than-honest mortgage loan brokers and home buyers) into taking full advantage.

Like any such event, things lined up perfectly to enable this, making what had seemed impossible very possible. Others have covered the details in ways that are not the focus here, especially books with marvelous titles such as *It Takes a Pillage* by Nomi Prins, *The Big Short* by Michael Lewis or *Fools Gold* by Gillian Tett. Films such as the Oscar-winning documentary *Inside Job* add their own interpretation. A very shortened version of events is as follows:

- Government regulation had been moving for some time in the US toward extending home ownership across a larger range of economic bands. People who had challenges affording the purchase of a house discovered that many of the obstacles they had previously found had been removed.
- This was partly enabled by a cheap money policy pushed by the Federal Reserve under Chairman Alan Greenspan, thereby lowering interest rates.
- US government entities such as those nicknamed "Fannie Mae" and "Freddie Mac"[3] enabled less fortunate people to have mortgages by buying them from the lenders who originated them.
- The financial services industry, *which had lobbied for years to be allowed to increase its "leverage,"* or the amount of capital required to back up its investments, had succeeded spectacularly in that endeavor and was at between 30 and 40:1, depending on the firm. That means for every $40 invested, only one dollar was their own capital, with $39 borrowed. By way of comparison, for most individuals, such leverage is limited to *one* pound, euro or dollar borrowed for every one of capital.
- The financial services industry in the US had also lobbied furiously for years to repeal the *Glass–Steagall Act*, which Congress had passed in two actions during the Great Depression (1932 and 1933) and which among other things separated investment banking (Wall Street) from deposit-taking banks (Main Street). It also created federal deposit insurance, which guaranteed the principal of consumer bank deposits up to a certain level. Part of this Act, of separating investment banking from deposit-taking banks, was repealed in 1999 and is widely believed to have contributed significantly to the 2008 Crash.[4]
- The reason for this belief about Glass–Steagall's partial repeal being a contributory factor in the Crash is that it allowed some Wall Street banks to gamble with Federally insured consumer deposits, and gamble they did. They also had the brilliant idea (at the time) to *securitize mortgages*, whereby these were bought in large quantities, packaged together and formed into a security like a bond that could be purchased by institutions. The ultimate owner of such mortgages would therefore often be thousands of miles and many countries distant from the homes for which the mortgages paid.
- Ratings agencies such as Standard & Poor's and Moody's were paid by the banks, who were selling these mortgage-backed securities, to rate the

financial quality of the securities on a scale starting at AAA for the very best. Many, if not all of these instruments, received the highest rating, even for mortgages that turned out to be worthless.

- Extremely smart people (especially those at AIG's now defunct Financial Products division in London) created new forms of insurance called CDSs (credit default swaps) which guaranteed the solvency of these mortgage-backed financial instruments, and such insurance was offered by AIG even though they seemed to know little about what they were insuring (AIG was bailed out by the US government, deemed "too big to fail," to the tune of a breathtaking *$150 billion*).
- Investors around the world, including sophisticated European banks, put their money into these instruments; after all, they were AAA rated, right?

If there was one way to summarize what had happened, it would be that government oversight of US banks had deteriorated to such a degree that the tail was now wagging the dog. Even some of the very people in government charged with regulating the financial services industry were refreshingly honest about this: as Spencer Bachus, the GOP chairman of the House Financial Services committee put it, government regulators "exist to serve banks."[5]

### Physics, chaos and the financial system

As we prepared to discuss the causes of the Crash here, we were curious as to whether such things are "inevitable," *perhaps part of the natural order of events in the universe.* To answer this question, we asked one of the top physicists in the world, Professor Sir John Enderby,[6] to tell us about how the laws of physics interpret the financial system and its effects on society. We chose a physicist because we noted that many physicists are employed in the finan-cial services industry, especially in areas such as high-speed trading, where nanoseconds make the difference between profit and loss, and in developing complex new financial products.[7] Sir John pointed out to us that the global financial system is "nonlinear," which means that in its natural, unregulated state it is *chaotic*; this is typified by the fact that Brazilian or Italian banks can have sudden and unpredictable effects on other banks worldwide. Lehman Brothers' 2008 demise comes to mind in this context. In a typical physics experiment, methods of *"damping,"* or controlling, a chaotic system are used to bring some order to this chaos, as Sir John explained to us, and in the financial sector, this damping consists of *regulation*. As damping increases, chaos is reduced, but so is growth; at some point, so much damping has been applied *that there is no longer any growth*. If we take just three stages of this in the following Chart 1.1, we see the relationship between damping, chaos and growth quite clearly:

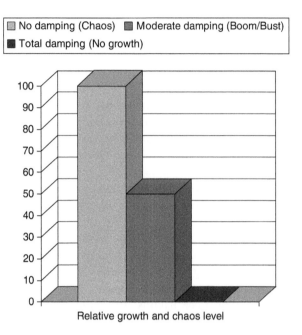

Chart 1.1   "Damping," Chaos and Growth

The challenge for the world's interconnected economy, as Sir John pointed out to us, is finding the right amount of regulation to ensure continued growth, but not too much to destroy that growth. *His main point was that a certain amount of chaos, the effects of which he calls "boom/bust," is inevitable to ensure growth.* This is a message that certain governments around the world, especially in Europe, might want to take to heart as they struggle with low growth. It also seems likely that damping of the US economic system, in the form of regulation, *was so loosened that it unleashed the chaos that ensued.*

## Causes of the Crash: Inside the organization

It is understandable that government often takes much of the blame for the Crash and its aftermath, and it certainly deserves plenty. As we saw earlier, it seems likely that the amount of "damping" in the US economy had been loosened and chaos ensued. However, *we believe that it would be a big mistake to place it all there.* Indeed, it would be a missed opportunity for us (meaning certainly the US and the UK, but also beyond that Anglo-American axis) if we did not take a *long, hard look inside our organizations for factors* that also contributed heavily to this event. If we ignore these, they will come back and bite us again, and next time we may not be so lucky as to have one of the world's top students of the

Great Depression at the helm of the US Federal Reserve, along with a team of gutsy individuals who were able to make the right decisions to prevent the ship from sinking. As much as it was to blame for some of this mess, then, the government was also the only entity that had the size and scope to rescue us from it.

When we step away from the government "blame game" we have the opportunity to ask something about some of our organizations: *what is it about them which is able to create such destruction?* Fortunately we have some courageous and insightful individuals who are starting to look in the mirror and not like what they see, even within the financial services industry. In what may be one of the most significant quotes in this book, James Gorman, CEO of one of the US banks that was hanging on to life by its fingernails in the autumn of 2008, Morgan Stanley, was quoted as saying something simple but extraordinarily powerful.

> Gorman, speaking at the Securities Industry and Financial Markets Association conference, said some individuals "who in many cases were frankly pretty average" made as much as 10 times that of people in other industries during the financial crisis … Fixing the culture will require "creating a compensation system that *better aligns or balances shareholders' interests and the broader society's interests with the individual's interests, and changing the perception that it's the individual that's the hero,*" Gorman, 52, said. "As an industry, we can have larger-than-life personalities, but individuals don't make institutions."[8]
>
> (emphasis added)

*"Don't make the individual the hero?"* As John McEnroe would have shouted to the umpire on Centre Court at Wimbledon, *"Surely you cannot be serious?"* The individual as hero is the mother's milk of Wall Street, it is the bedrock of financial sectors from New York to the City of London, Frankfurt, Paris and Shanghai; central to the rugged individualism of this industry and core to its culture! Yet there he was, suggesting that that has to change. Interestingly, right after Lehman Brothers failed in September 2008, Morgan Stanley was the target of the short sellers and barely escaped with its life. Gorman was not CEO at the time,[9] but was brought in later to turn things around, which is perhaps why we are hearing this from him and not from any incumbents who were in place when the Crash occurred.

*"Aligning or balancing shareholders' interests and the broader society's interests with the individual's interests?"* Again, McEnroe would be apoplectically screaming at the umpire up in his high chair! Since when does Wall Street have to worry about "society"? It's all about the next bonus and that in turn is all about the next deal. *Shareholders?* Do you mean those people who own the shares and therefore own the company, but who are allowed very little say on important things such as executive compensation?

Mr. Gorman is right of course, and he has stuck his neck out and given us a blueprint for change, even with such a short quote. Perhaps being an Australian and not having spent his whole career on Wall Street[10] gives him the chance to look beyond the normal operating procedures and culture of the "Street" and bring a fresh, outside perspective. One day we might all look back and thank him that his words helped us move in a different direction, one in which we no longer lurch from one catastrophe to another. After all, 2008 was barely 25 years after the US "Savings and Loan crisis" in which hundreds of banks went under, massive amounts of taxpayer rescue money was funneled into the (yes!) financial services industry, and systemic risk was high. These events are not without consequence and do not always end well: Japan had its own such real-estate bubble shortly thereafter and there is some evidence that it has never fully recovered even all these years later.

James Gorman's quote therefore leads us into the role played by our organizations in the Crash. If we can understand the mechanisms operating there, we can start to see how those can be changed. To do this we first need to look at the "culture" at work, since culture is what determines whether the organization focuses equally or unequally on society, its shareholders, the welfare of its suppliers, its workers as a whole or just its individual "heroes."

## Organization culture

Organizational culture is an immensely important and interesting subject, which will be our focus for much of this book, as we attempt to explain the organizational contribution to the Crash and to factors that either *hold us back at work, or propel us forward*. There is a simple and workable definition of culture in our organizations, which has stood the test of time, and it is this:

> The way we do things around here.[11,12]

According to this definition, culture (how we "*do*" things) is a set of *behaviors*; these are driven in turn by *values* held by leadership. In the financial services industry, it is generally accepted that the cultures of the member firms are hard driving, individual ("hero," "star") oriented, always on the knife-edge, much like the businesses they are in. Firms like Morgan Stanley and Goldman Sachs make their money from trading, from being brokers for others who trade, from advising companies on mergers/acquisitions and from listing new companies on stock exchanges, among other things. These are all fiercely competitive activities, and many might say that such internal cultures are not only justified but absolutely necessary to achieve their mission. However, the low tide of the Crash exposed the dark side of the culture of these companies.

## Ethics at the individual and corporate level

There is nothing about the culture of financial services firms, which we have described previously, which would automatically make them undertake activities that would lead to the Crash. Being hard charging and aggressive is something that is prized in many areas, for example, in sports. We expect that a football game will be played according to the rules, that those rules will be enforced, and that the best team will win. But that is not what happened here; what happened is that we had a years-long "game" in which many of the *referees and other officials seemed to be in a bar across the street from the field*, for part of the time the game was being played. Not only that, but some of the rules of the game had been rewritten shortly before it started, as a result of fierce lobbying by the players and owners! Should we then be surprised that the game was then played in a less than "fair" way?

For example, mortgage brokers (some of whom we know personally) were able to move into the relative regulatory vacuum, into an environment some would say had been "socially engineered" for failure, and sell mortgages to severely under-qualified individuals, knowing full well that those people would almost certainly default. This behavior has a name: *unethical*. Talking with such people about the mechanics of a transaction, it is not surprising that, when multiplied millions of times, the Crash had to happen. For example, certain loans in the US were designated as not requiring proof of income and this was quite legal. This meant that a game could be played between broker and borrower, perhaps involving nonverbal cues like nods and winks, and sounding something like this:

BROKER:    So your income is ... what did you say ... $80,000 a year?
BORROWER:  Not that much.
BROKER:    But if we say $80,000, it would not be so far off would it?
BORROWER:  Is that what it will take to get this loan?
BROKER:    Exactly, we need $80,000.
BORROWER:  OK then, if that's what we need to say.

While this is made up, it is almost verbatim from what we have been told was the case by people in the industry.

Now depending on one's religious or spiritual background, or perhaps an upbringing that may have not involved any religion but instead involved strong lessons in ethical behavior, this sounds outrageous. But it is only the tip of the iceberg as far as the Crash of 2008 is concerned. Others at the top of this food chain—let's call them the sharks—had their own version of unethical behavior, which made the mortgage brokers look like minnows.

Let's consider the behavior of Goldman Sachs (GS), as outlined in a fraud case against the firm developed by the Securities and Exchange Commission (SEC) which resulted in the *largest fine ever leveled by that agency against a Wall Street firm ($550 million)*.[13] While the case is complex, its details and outcome are extraordinary in the insight they give us into the Crash. GS was accused of fraud because in working with a hedge fund client, Paulson and Company, to develop a financial instrument that contained multiple mortgages (a so-called collateralized debt obligation or CDO), and subsequently selling that CDO to investors, *it left out what would have been some rather useful information for the buyers*. The structure of this deal was that Paulson would sell the CDO "short", betting on it losing value, while the investors would hold it "long" for income and capital gain purposes. The investors were not neophytes but sophisticated organizations such as IKB Deutsche Industriebank, which normally work hard to make sure that their investment is a good one (so-called due diligence); however, such work is possible only when one has all the information about what one is buying. In this case the buyers were told only that another firm (not Paulson) had selected the exact items to be included in the CDO "package," whereas in fact the very firm shorting this instrument, Paulson, had had a big hand at selecting them! Now one does not need a degree in business or psychology to know that the short seller might be tempted to pack some less than perfect material into something that he wanted to go downhill, and downhill it went. Paulson made $1 billion in this transaction, and the investors lost that money. Paulson was not charged by the SEC because it was not his job to disclose his work in selecting the content of the CDO to the sellers; that was GS's job.

If your eyes glazed over with the details of this affair, then we can let the SEC people explain in their damningly straightforward words the basis of their charges and the settlement that was reached:

> "Half a billion dollars is the largest penalty ever assessed against a financial services firm in the history of the SEC," said Robert Khuzami, Director of the SEC's Division of Enforcement. "This settlement is a stark lesson to Wall Street firms that no product is too complex, and no investor too sophisticated, to avoid a heavy price *if a firm violates the fundamental principles of honest treatment and fair dealing.*"
>
> Lorin L. Reisner, Deputy Director of the SEC's Division of Enforcement, added, "The unmistakable message of this lawsuit and today's settlement is that half-truths and deception cannot be tolerated and that the integrity of the securities markets depends on all market participants acting with *uncompromising adherence to the requirements of truthfulness and honesty.*"[14]
>
> (emphasis added)

How interesting that the government regulators used such words as "honesty," "truthfulness" and "fairness" in their criticism of GS. As we shall see later, these words form not only the basis of the "integrity of securities markets" as the SEC said but are also the bedrock of day-to-day business transactions around the world and of something with equal significance: *worker morale and engagement, in every organization.*

As the Nobel Prize-winning economist Joseph E. Stiglitz has pointed out when summarizing the effects of the Crash, these moral and ethical aspects as well as the effects on society as a whole should be front and center as we discuss what happened:

> Too little has been written about the underlying moral deficit that has been exposed—a deficit that is larger, and harder to correct ... We have created a society in which materialism overwhelms moral commitment, in which the rapid growth that we have achieved is not sustainable environmentally or socially, *in which we do not act together to address our common needs.* Market fundamentalism has eroded any sense of community ... There has been an erosion of trust—and not just in our financial institutions. It is not too late to close these fissures.[15]
>
> (emphasis added)

## Fallout from the Crash

### Economic effects

No event like the Crash of 2008, with its size and scope, could fail to have an enormous effect on society as a whole and on organizations in particular. Job losses throughout the world resulting from the Crash have been widely publicized; *in the US alone some eight million jobs were lost from peak to trough.* US unemployment doubled to above 10% in some places and above 9% on average (12.5% in the country's most populous state, California). Many of these jobs are not expected to come back soon, or ever, given that they were dependent on the very conditions that lead to the Crash itself (cheap money, easily obtained mortgages, etc.). These included jobs in real estate sales, mortgage loan origination, home construction and related professions. In the UK, job losses were very steep and may not have troughed (in 2011) due to massive spending cuts announced by the new Conservative-Liberal coalition government, which will significantly affect public employment. Continental Europe has had mixed results, with Portugal, Ireland, Italy, Greece and Spain (so-called, and unfortunately named, PIIGS) hard-hit by a debt crisis exacerbated by the Crash, and Germany essentially acting as the banker of last resort to prop up the euro. Housing markets in places like Spain have been devastated as they have throughout the US, with average prices down about 40–50% from the 2006 peak. Many banks have closed or been merged into nonexistence. Spectacular Crashes have occurred in the UK (Northern Rock and Royal Bank of Scotland became wards of the state), and in places like Iceland, where UK and

Dutch savers chased temptingly high yields, both they and their over-generous banks went off the cliff. Others have had to be propped up or merged due to ingestion of many toxic assets generated by the alchemists on Wall Street (the state-owned and -operated Landesbank system in Germany, for example).

Unemployment moved up in Europe, but Germany managed, in spite of its banking exposure, to re-emerge quickly thanks to its powerhouse export industries and the hunger for their output of cars and other items in places not affected by the Crash. As a result it has been seeing record low unemployment as China buys as many Audis, BMWs, Volkswagens and Mercedes as the Germans can build.

### Criminal proceedings or lack thereof

To date no one has gone to jail for any activity directly related to this Crash, prompting an interesting article titled, *"Why isn't Wall Street in Jail?"* from someone who has written in depth of the subject, Matt Taibbi of *Rolling Stone*.[16] As Taibbi points out, only Bernie Madoff, he of the massive hedge fund scandal, has gone to jail during the time period of the Crash, but Madoff himself had nothing to do with that Crash! Taibbi's analysis of the cozy relationship between Wall Street and its regulators is devastating. He quotes simple facts about personnel at the main Wall Street regulator, the Securities and Exchange Commission (SEC), to set the stage for the inevitable conclusion:

> The Revolving Door isn't just a footnote in financial law enforcement; over the past decade, more than a dozen high-ranking SEC officials have gone on to lucrative jobs at Wall Street banks or white-shoe law firms, where partnerships are worth millions.

This connection leads Taibbi to conclude that, essentially, the game is fixed:

> The mental stumbling block, for most Americans, is that financial crimes don't feel real; you don't see the culprits waving guns in liquor stores ... But these frauds are worse than common robberies. They're crimes of intellectual choice, made by people ... acting on a simple, cynical calculation: Let's steal whatever we can, then dare the victims to find the juice to reclaim their money through a captive bureaucracy.

To the average criminal languishing in the vast US prison system for (relatively) small scale theft or fraud, there must be a cruel sense of irony and unfairness about the system that allows Wall Street to get away with outright fraud and destruction of jobs and lives, and not have to pay the price. As we saw in the case of Goldman Sachs, when a price is paid it is usually in the form of a deal, whereby no guilt is admitted and *shareholders, not executives, foot the bill for the fine.*

## Political effects

Predictably it was new regulation that was the knee-jerk reaction for certain members of the US Congress, and public anger was enough to persuade plenty of members to vote in favor. This was not a totally misguided effort, since areas of activity in financial services had been exposed, which were so new and outside the radar range of then-current regulation that they had to be covered. There was plenty of hand wringing, too, about lack of implementation of current regulation, especially about the enforcers of that regulation, the SEC, being "asleep at the wheel." New US laws passed in 2010 will theoretically break up failing financial institutions previously "too big to fail" and will force many of the transactions involving exotic financial instruments out of the darkness and into the light of exchanges. Outside the US, France passed new laws to rein in excesses.[17] Whether all this will change human behavior or not, remains to be seen; in particular, the big question is whether the fine balance can be maintained between necessary control and heavy-handed and economically depressing government intervention ("damping" as Professor Enderby calls it). Will tightening on Wall Street and elsewhere kill the golden goose of risk taking and the other crucial underpinnings of capitalism? Will there be an "overshoot" effect, which, by trying the control the excesses (and perhaps to punish the perpetrators by clamping down on their playground), ends up hurting the basis of the capitalist economies?

While it is clear from examining the mechanics of the Crash that Wall Street firms were responsible for a significant portion of it (and individuals there benefited hugely as a result of it, as we see later), what is so interesting is how the public has given them a pass. Searching for political fallout, few if any people were seen demonstrating in US streets soon after the Crash, with any sense of outrage, *specifically about Wall Street behavior.* Why is this? Perhaps because the events that lead to the Crash were like a big party, which many attended; from the financial companies to individual homeowners, cheap money and easily obtained mortgages meant that the party was not only big but long-lasting. Somewhere inside, many people know that they too were part of the problem. In the US and elsewhere, during the period 2000 to 2007, homeowners could see huge increases in the value of their homes and their resulting net worth, and they took advantage of this by continually refinancing, using their homes as virtual bank cash machines.

Polling data cited next shows quite clearly one of the reasons for the lack of anger at the financial services industry, which is that, aside from public self-blame, Wall Street has a foil—*the US government*:

> Since 1965, Gallup has asked survey respondents to choose the biggest future threat to the country: big business, big labor, or big government. Big government always wins—by a lot. In December 2006, 61 percent said they

fretted about the government, compared with 25 percent who feared corporate power. [In the spring of 2009], when Wall Street was in deep disrepute, the numbers changed only slightly: 55 percent still fingered big government as the greatest threat.[18]

Public anger was there all right: the rise of the Tea Party, and their rallies which accompanied the mid-term elections of 2010, followed by huge success at the polls, demonstrated exactly those feelings against government, which the Gallup poll mentioned before has measured. What is so interesting about this is the underlying value system that the Tea Party's success uncovers, and which can be described with one word: *karma*. In a fascinating article[19] titled *"What the Tea Partiers Really Want," The Wall Street Journal* set out as clear a picture of this powerful political movement as any we have seen. Essentially it stated that karma (not the Hindu spiritual version but more of a homegrown one not related to any religious beliefs) had been violated yet again during the Crash; this had happened because actions (*karma* in Sanskrit means *"action"*) had been separated from their consequences, and government had a lot to do with it. As the Journal pointed out:

> [S]uppose you learned that politicians were devising policies that might, as a side effect of their enactment, nullify the law of karma. Bad deeds would no longer lead to bad outcomes, and the fragile moral order of our nation would break apart. For tea partiers, this scenario is not science fiction. It is the last 80 years of American history ... Now jump ahead to today's ongoing financial and economic crisis. Again, those guilty of corruption and irresponsibility have escaped the consequences of their wrongdoing, rescued first by President Bush and then by President Obama. Bailouts and bonuses sent unimaginable sums of the taxpayers' money to the very people who brought calamity upon the rest of us. Where is punishment for the wicked?[20]

The Tea Partiers have a point, which many can get behind. It is also something which crosses political lines because when one talks to people from all walks of life in the United States there is a tangible *sense of unfairness* surrounding this Crash, no matter which party they support. As Joseph Stiglitz, someone politically far from the Tea Party, says:

> Part of moral behavior and individual responsibility is to accept blame when it is due. Yet bankers have repeatedly worked hard to shift blame to others, including to those they victimized. In today's financial markets, almost everyone claims innocence. They were all just doing their jobs. There was individualism, but no individual responsibility.[21]

One of the best phrases which has been bandied around, and which summarizes this view concisely, is that the financial firms of Wall Street have:

> privatized profits and socialized losses.[22]

Is the Tea Party (even if some of its followers have crazy ideas on fringes of the movement[23]) doing us all a favor by *demanding a sense of fairness* in having a moral balancing-out of these accounts and making people accountable for their actions? We believe it is and we will build on this karma-based viewpoint of fairness later in this book.

## Changes in education practices

It is not a big jump from the events of 2008–2010 to an examination of the education of those responsible, and the possibility that changes in that area might come about which would spare us from future "Masters of the Universe." Such a thing has happened, and at no less a hallowed institution than Harvard Business School[24]:

> The university caused a stir last week when it said it would significantly revamp its M.B.A. program, adding new required courses with an increased focus on *ethics and teamwork* … "The public lost trust in business, and some of our graduates seem to be responsible for that," says Nitin Nohria, who was appointed dean of the school in July 2010.
>
> (emphasis added)

Dean Nohria's refreshingly honest and open statement is encouraging for a number of reasons: first he actually takes responsibility for his organization having played a role in the Crash *via its own graduates*. Secondly, key elements that we have identified earlier as contributing to the organizational side of the ledger when it came to this Crash—teamwork and ethics—are the focus of the changes to the MBA curriculum. As Harvard moves forward with this, we hope that MBA students there and elsewhere will create some *balance* by focusing more on "we" and less on "me," and do so in a more ethical way than Dean Nohria indicates some of their alumni have done. Such a shift in focus will inoculate us from *Crash 2008: The Sequel*, a film that we cannot afford to make. As we have seen in the very recent past, it is not too dramatic to say that our future might depend on whether and how we change.

# 2
# A Benefit of the Crash: More Focus on Culture and Engagement at Work

They say that "every cloud has a silver lining." Is there a silver lining to the Crash, one which will help us move forward? We believe there is a huge one: as we have seen on Wall Street, the Crash was like an earthquake which has exposed the fault lines in some of our organizational cultures and forced us to ask questions about how we manage them. If we are smart about what we do with this information, *and we have the courage to change*, perhaps the probability of the next Crash can be at least lessened, *and that would be only the start*. When we look at the cultures within our organizations, we cannot help but wonder how they affect day-to-day work life for hundreds of millions of people who work in them. To give just one example, if the "individual is hero," how does that affect people who might be very good at their jobs but very poor at being "heroes"?

To examine these issues we have to look at what culture is within an organization, how it comes about and how it ultimately will determine whether or not our workers *engage*. This is a topic that is enjoying an explosion of attention around the world, from government reports on the subject, to fast-growing online communities, and for very good reason:

> Work environments can be much improved, workers' lives can be *healthier and happier*, our productivity can be raised and our standard of living protected ... at the very least ... if we become far more conscious at managing the culture, or "the way we do things" at work. Specifically, if we make that culture much more "engagement-friendly."

## Culture at work: Driving our organizations

As we have seen, culture is simply defined in this book by "the way we do things around here." This definition has stood the test of time and does not depend on complex "academic-speak" to understand or communicate throughout our organizations. For this reason we have always recommended it to clients who want to openly and actively start a dialogue with their workforce on this topic.

Culture at work is such an interesting and valuable topic because it is often a hidden and powerful force, which drives how many things happen. Since it is about behavior ("the way we *do* things") it can be measured and it can be changed. We often have the experience that leaders become intensely interested in this subject when they find out how much it explains about what happens at work, whether and how they can change things, and so on. How many times have we read that two companies combined but were not able to be successful because of a "clash of cultures"?[1]

## A model of organizational culture and engagement

Work culture and the worker engagement, which results from it or not, is forged from potent sources of influence, which we have set out in visual form in the model which follows:

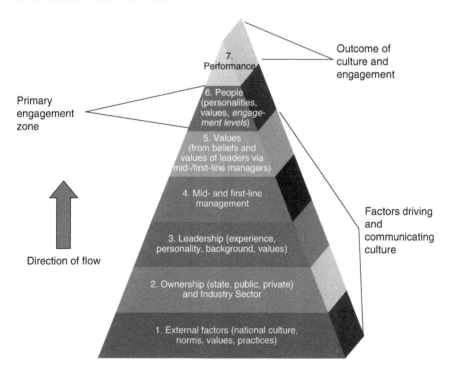

*Chart 2.1*　A model of organization culture and engagement

If our model looks like a Maslow pyramid, it is not a coincidence, since they work in the same way: in Maslow's model, basic human needs were at the bottom of the pyramid and had to be met before one could move upward to things like self-actualization. Similarly, in our model, the lower-level elements influence those above them, and all elements come together, to

- Create the culture of the organization
- Determine the extent to which worker engagement will happen
- Significantly influence the achievement of the organizational mission ("performance")

Now we *are not saying that culture is the only driver of performance*. Clearly, if your finances are not in good order or you make serious strategic or marketing mistakes, performance will take a big hit. But culture and its by-product, engagement, do find their way into so much of an organization's workings: for example, a disengaged and disgruntled marketing team is unlikely to produce stellar results.

Let's take a trip from bottom to top and see how the organization's culture develops, how workers respond to that culture, and ultimately how the organization *performs*.

### Level 1: External factors (national culture, norms, values, practices)

So many organizations operate inside just one country that we cannot ignore that country's values and culture as an influence on them. Let's take Germany, where one might still use the formal *Sie* (you) with the lady who owns the guesthouse where you have spent the last 20 summer holidays, whereas in California you would have been on first-name terms either immediately or shortly after day one. This formality tends to carry over into the workplace, and we are going to find out later how it affects engagement in that country. Let's just say, not positively! Cultural norms weigh heavily in such places as France, where one would not dream of paying a CEO like he would be paid in the US, for example. Norms can change: in Japan, lifetime job security used to be the norm until the real estate crash starting in 1990 and the "Lost Decade" (now more like two decades). Now it is gone and engagement has gone along with it. With the death of Princess Diana in 1997, there was a striking example of how national culture can shift: the muted emotional tone one would normally expect from the British people was shattered by the magnitude of feeling for Diana, and there was an outpouring that neither of us had seen in our decades there. However, when the Queen first reacted she was seen as woefully out of touch with that heightened emotional flow; only when she appeared on television, (atypically) in front of a Buckingham Palace window, and presented a softer face to the British people, did she come back in tune with what had been a major shift. The recent Prince William-Kate Middleton wedding underscored how much this shift was not temporary, but has now become part of a "new monarchy" in the UK.

This country-specific cultural effect is very much modified by the extent to which an organization has moved beyond its national boundaries and taken on an international focus. The "home-country" culture then becomes quite diluted—for example, its own language may not even be spoken by many of those working at HQ. For example, some multinational organizations with which we have experience in the German-speaking countries have implemented English as a worldwide standard for management and have imported US-style first-name use along with the language. This can be a powerful cultural statement and changes a formal culture in ways that can make it much more "engagement-friendly." This and other practices necessary to operate around the world further undermine the unique culture of the country where they may still be based, but which no longer drives everything about the "way they do things." If we were to describe Nestlé, for example, just in terms of its management style and practices, its scope and revenue, would there be anything about it that made it absolutely, definitely Swiss? Probably not, until we told you that one of its major products is chocolate, and even then.

## Level 2: Ownership and industry sector

*Ownership and work culture*

Some countries maintain a high level of state ownership that also has a huge effect on organizations there. Let's imagine a company partly owned by the People's Liberation Army in China (as more than a few are) and a stockholder-owned one in the same business in the UK; the differences at the societal level—beginning with the differences between the countries and their cultures and histories, let alone the ownership of the enterprise—are enormous and will affect every aspect of the organizations, including their level of worker engagement. Or take the example of a community-owned and -operated hospital in the Munich area of Germany and compare that to a for-profit hospital somewhere in the US: the cultures are very different; take it from one of us who has had the exact same operation in each! The for-profit, hounded by a private insurance company, which was paying for it, kicked us out after one night; the community-owned German hospital had to be begged to let us leave after six nights, since the standard there was eight.

Private companies can be quite different places to work, culturally, than those which are publicly owned (e.g., by shareholders). On the one hand, some can be very informal and have far less pressure due to not having to report endlessly increasing earnings every quarter to the markets. On the other hand, what if you work there and have to compete with a family member who you believe is in his job simply because of the good fortune of his last name? Issues of favoritism and nepotism come up often in these environments, and how the culture treats them will be sure to affect its success.

*Industry sector and culture*

An organization culture that might be successful in one industry could be a disaster in another. We would expect a hard-charging and risk-taking culture to be prevalent in the financial services industry (but with some changes to which we have already alluded) but such a culture would be bad news for the operators of nuclear power plants or hospitals. In the hospital, strict adherence to rules and procedures (such as infection control, triage, etc.) are key; not that the culture of medicine is one of no risk, but it is a carefully controlled risk. So we see the need to match the culture to the business one is in, leaving room for the unique features that leadership always brings to the table. This is why Dell is not Apple and Virgin Atlantic is not British Airways.

## Level 3: Leadership

An organization's culture rests on the shoulders of its top leaders, whether or not they created it in the first place.

If an organization wants to change its culture, it usually must change its leader(s). Time and again, we have seen new leaders come into organizations and completely turn around their cultures and their organization's performance. We have also seen new start-ups forge what are clearly high engagement cultures from scratch, because of their leaders' vision, force of personality and the most important (and most misused) factor of all: *values*. The background and experiences of leaders forges a great deal of what will become the core culture for an organization. Walmart is often mentioned in this context because it has been so successful; founder Sam Walton was a frugal person whose frugality to this day dominates Walmart's culture. Founders such as Walton and Thomas J. Watson Sr. at IBM can have great effect even after death; one of us experienced that as a young summer intern at IBM's UK Laboratories near Winchester, England, where the Watson-mandated dark suit, white shirt and "sincere" tie was very much *de rigueur* in those days. In time it changes, as IBM indeed did.[2] John Mackey's early life as a hippie has shaped the culture of Whole Foods from day one, making it employee-friendly in ways that other US grocery stores did not. Similarly Sir Terry Leahy's background shaped the culture at UK grocery powerhouse Tesco and brought it enormous success as a result:

> The business does reflect Sir Terry's personality ... His humble origins are evident in the openness of the culture. By creating the Finest and the Value ranges, he sent a message that everyone is welcome.[3]

Leaders do make a big difference and set the tone but in larger organizations their effectiveness is moderated by much more limited access to those who form the vast majority of the workforce. Not every company can enjoy pizza all together in the CEO's back garden. In those larger organizations, which sometimes employ many people nationally or around the world, it is mid- and first-line management, which is that crucial *cultural bridge*.

## Level 4: Mid- and first-line management

Individuals who are hired into the position of *first-line management, supervisor, team leader* or whatever the organization uses to denote this level are the key link between the organizational leadership, its culture and values and the people who make up the non-management ranks. In larger organizations "higher" levels of managers are also in place between here and the C-suite and are also crucial to engagement, being part of the information flow and the implementation of cultural norms. But it is the first-line level that repeatedly emerges as the *deciding factor in whether an organization is able to create a cultural environment in which workers wish to engage*.

## Level 5: Values

With leadership and management levels, we looked at the *structure* of the organization and its relationship to organizational culture. But no culture comes into existence via structure alone: instead *values* breathe life into the structure and shape how things will be done. Values are one of the most important factors in any organizational culture and *those values start at the top*. Every organization has values whether they are written down or not. Some values are distributed widely and not just within the organization: for example, on every Starbucks Coffee Company cup and sleeve there are statements about the company's commitment to "doing business in ways that are good to each other, coffee farmers and the planet." Other organizations may have values that are unwritten and even unspoken but drive the internal culture nonetheless. The fact that some organizations have values that are regularly expressed verbally, written down and distributed widely such as on materials used by customers or in annual reports, does not always mean much: *those values may not be lived at all.* Not uncommon is the company that states a particular value, but when we have surveyed those people, we find just the opposite. Such things can make one cynical, and can also be the subject of wickedly accurate cartoons such as that by Garry Trudeau's *Doonesbury*, which is well worth a click-through due to its timely connection to the financial services Crash![4] *Values, then, are easier said than done.*

*Leadership values: Where are they from and how do they work?*

Here we step briefly into the world of psychology. Values are sets of beliefs about the world, not always conscious: *they drive how we behave.* For example, if we believe people are basically good, we will treat them that way. If we believe they are lazy and not so good, we will treat them totally differently. These things sound very simple but it is surprising how many managers are not so conscious of this in themselves. This lack of consciousness can make these beliefs very hard to change; they started in childhood and were reinforced for a long time then. *Every relationship is affected by them, outside and inside the workplace.*

Of course, beliefs about people go far beyond whether they are basically "good" or "bad"; the beliefs most in effect at work have to do with whether people need to be coaxed into working hard, or have a natural drive to do so. Whether they need to be guided through every step of what they do, or just given goals and be left to do "their own thing." Often these beliefs are so ingrained that they are *applied to all people*, regardless of whether or not that person really "fits the mold." As they say, *for a hammer, everything is a nail.*

Values work best when they are stated both in general terms and also in terms of *expected behaviors*. You need to make it clear what these values look like when they are lived. That way, they can be measured in the organization and incorporated into both manager and worker goals, as we shall see later.

### Values and mid- to first-line management

Forged from the values of leadership and the means by which the values are actualized in the organization, *the culture or "way we do things" becomes the behavioral version of these values.* While leaders may "set the tone" here, *it is first-level managers who carry this message forward with their day-to-day behavior and the relationships they create with their teams.* They are the frontline guides on the "culture journey" of an organization, which means they had better be good at this job; so much depends on it.

### Typical values that organizations cite

We have all seen the statements that companies put in their Annual Reports and other corporate communications, such as *"People are our most valuable asset!"*

This is a value statement, albeit with a kind of wording that some now see as outmoded. The reason is that some complain that people aren't an "asset" or a "resource" at all, which places us on the same level as computer chips or natural gas reserves. Value statements about "people" have more recently been leaving these words out, which are themselves value statements. We now see business cards with the title "Head of People" now instead of "VP Human Resources." Often value statements appear next to Mission Statements, which is a good idea since those values are the means by which the Mission Statement is going to be made real and more than a statement. Listen to both of these from Hilti Group, the construction technology company in Liechtenstein, an organization of which we are big fans, which has consistently high morale, engagement and performance, and which we featured in *Employee Morale:*[5]

> *Mission Statement:* We passionately create enthusiastic customers and build a better future.
> *Our Values:* Integrity, courage, teamwork and commitment.[6]

Hilti's web site then goes on to "flesh out" these values and to explain how they are lived, by placing them all into one sentence, preceded with a statement that precisely summarizes what we have said here about the nature of the values-culture link:

> The way we do things at Hilti is based on living strong values. We act with *integrity* in all we do, we demonstrate *courage* to go beyond the circle of habits, we outperform through *teamwork*, and we have *commitment* to personal and company growth.[7]

Sometimes a simple value statement becomes the *mantra*, which not only guides a company's employees but becomes the basis on which its customers see its products. Consider Apple's Steve Jobs (who sadly passed away while this book was being written) and the phrase he has always been quoted as using in this context: "insanely great."[8] Judging by the lines that form outside Apple stores worldwide when a new "must-have" device is released, customers seem to believe that Jobs delivered on this promise. No doubt this phrase has been in more than one Apple engineer's head as she labored over the next iteration of the iPhone, MacBook Pro or iPad!

Google has placed its values into a philosophy, which has not changed too much over the years since its founding, probably because: (1) Its founders are still there, in fact one of them just retook the CEO spot from a non-founder[9] and (2) This philosophy has made them extremely successful, so why change? Google's philosophy includes the following:

- Focus on the user and all else will follow.
- It's best to do one thing really, really well.
- You can make money without doing evil.
- You can be serious without a suit.
- Great just isn't good enough.[10]

Sometimes values simply pop out on the radar screen as something quite unusual and (whether one agrees with them or not) powerful. Consider the following value statement from Vineet Nayar, CEO of India-based HCL Technologies, a company with no less than 60,000 employees: *Employees First, Customers Second*.

One of us heard him speak at a large international conference held by the Society for Human Resource Management (SHRM),[11] where he talked about this value and the book that has the aforesaid value statement as its title. On the book cover, management guru Tom Peters does not hide his enthusiasm for Mr. Nayar or his values:

> Rumor is that Vineet Nayar has invented a whole new way of configuring and managing an enterprise. I think there's more than a grain of truth to

that. I'm on the verge of the verge of declaring that Mr. Nayar could be the next Peter Drucker[12]

Of course, Mr. Nayar is not the first to "flip" the organization chart over on its head; this is not the new part of his statement, it is the customer part that is so blatantly stated and new. Not everyone buys into this value statement: a second keynote speaker at the same conference the next day, Marcus Buckingham, said he respected Mr. Nayar but disagreed entirely with that particular part of his philosophy. Nonetheless, it does show that some consider employees so important that they are on a completely different level than customers. Perhaps no one else at the top of other organizations has the courage to say this and possibly offend their customers, even though it might make sense: without a people-oriented culture that drives high employee morale and engagement, customers will be less well served, as so much research has shown.[13]

### Values and brand

Values and brand are cousins, in that brands are often built on the underlying values of the organization. Brands are often said to have "brand values," which build an emotional connection with customers and other stakeholders.[14] The result over time is "reputation," a "valuable" thing to have when it is good. Considering how much organizations invest in the brand and their reputation, it is not surprising that they will go to any length to defend it. Listen to Warren Buffett, CEO of Berkshire Hathaway and one of the most quoted organizational leaders anywhere[15]:

> Lose money for the firm and I will be understanding; lose a shred of reputation for the firm, and I will be ruthless.[16]

### How values contribute to organizational culture

Imagine you go into a corporate lobby and are "welcomed" by a plastic plant, no chairs and a telephone on the wall with a rather curt note to call an operator. Welcome to their culture! Or you go in and find a marble floor, nice art on the walls, real plants and a friendly receptionist ready to pour you some coffee and let your host know you are here. Either way, you already know quite a bit about this organization: what it values, how it wishes to be seen, how much it cares about "image," etc. Sometimes first impressions tell you what you might not wish to know: as the old joke goes, *"never go to a doctor whose lobby plants are dead."*

All this derives from the organization's values and those values flow into whether the plant is plastic or not and the receptionist real or just a phone. Beyond the lobby, every single one of these beliefs and values will affect not just the physical environment but also the psychological one: *how leaders and managers treat their people, day in and day out.* This is what we refer to as the "culture" of the organization, or "how things are done," such as:

- Who is hired and promoted
- How people are paid
- Management style, such as authoritarian and command and control or more liberal
- The sense of urgency in how things are done
- The focus on customer satisfaction
- The focus on quality
- The focus on community support and involvement
- What kinds of behaviors are celebrated and rewarded by the organization
- Teamwork versus individual focus

In the past, many organizations had unwritten values that essentially drove their behavior through example, reward structures, promotions, selective hiring and so on. Increasingly, though, organizations see the importance of values and of extending these in a *conscious way* throughout the organization. While this is often a "top-down" exercise (such as at a company that had a charismatic founder whose values are still followed rather like a religion), it is often a valuable exercise to use extensive input from all levels of the workforce to at least discuss the values and have some input to them.[17]

## Level 6: People

There is a reason why companies increasingly spend so much time on recruitment: that person you bring into the organization becomes part of the culture going forward, that same culture which has been created by influences from Levels 1 to 5 in our model. Do they extend the culture in a positive way or push against it and create a small, but not insignificant, crack? The culture is so significant and *consciously managed* at Whole Foods, for example, that team members must vote on someone who is a candidate to join their team. No "dumping" someone on them who will become toxic to what they, as a team, have built and nurture every day with their behavior. Google does the same with team members and managers alike. This is a fundamental statement that *culture is the basis of who we are and what we do and we will do whatever we can to protect it.*

As a living and breathing thing, culture therefore *both affects and depends on whom you bring into it.* Far better to take the time and pick someone who will fully support your culture from day one, rather than compromising and think that that person will "come around" with time. Smart organizations know this and go far beyond talent and skills in their recruitment activities. Picking the right people to work for you, and picking or promoting the right ones as managers, coaches, supervisors, mentors, whatever you call them, is a crucial *cultural effort* that will pay big dividends going forward. It will be an incredibly important determinant of whether your organization's culture can be successful.

When the factors driving culture in the organization reach the workforce, *the stage is set for whether those people will engage or not*, which is something we will expand on extensively further. This in turn will serve to enhance—or detract from—the performance of your organization.

**Level 7: Performance**

We mentioned before that we are not naïve enough to believe that a great work culture is *sufficient* to drive performance, absent a good financial condition or a robust and effective strategy. It is, however, *necessary* to make it happen. Culture will determine whether a great strategy can be *implemented* instead of it just sitting on a shelf in a three-ring binder. Exactly how this capability works is something we will now discuss.

Culture is therefore built from a combination of influences from Levels 1 to 5 in our model and communicated directly to the workforce (through formal internal communications) and indirectly (through HR practices and the behavior of leaders, mid- and first-level managers, who are watched carefully for the messages they deliver). Based on what workers see and experience day in and day out, *they choose to engage with the organization to a greater or lesser extent*.

## From culture to worker engagement: The choice that powers performance

By now most organizations around the world have at least heard of worker engagement and have some understanding of its significance. Some have fully embraced the concept and work hard every day to build a culture that will support it. Others remain skeptical that this is worth the effort and cost. For example, David MacLeod in the UK, leader of a group that studied the subject of engagement for the government there,[18] recently (2010) shared research that found

> [m]ore than half of (UK) CEOs are not engaged in engagement ... 22% do not understand the concept, 19.2% are not aware of the business benefits and 14.5% are aware of the concept, but do not believe there will be any ROI.[19]

Hopefully, MacLeod and his colleagues' valuable work and excellent report, released in 2009, will drive these numbers higher. There certainly is room for improvement, and in light of what we now know about the performance benefits, the UK (and elsewhere) would be well advised to go down this road. We did our best to add to this conversation by covering this subject in some detail, specifically focusing on the performance aspects of morale in our 2009 book.[20] At this point there is no question that the evidence in favor of high morale and its cousin, engagement, being not only correlated with performance, *but also driving it*, is overwhelming. As a result of this, the most sophisticated organizations worldwide make great efforts to measure, identify and manage engagement levels.[21] *They know that an engaged workforce is far, far more than "nice to have"; it is "mission critical."*

## What is engagement?

First of all, engagement is a *behavior,* something people at work *do* to a greater or lesser extent. Morale is, on the other hand, an inner state of well-being belonging to an individual or group.[22] Morale and engagement are related in that high morale makes it much more likely that people will engage with the organization and their jobs. It is important to make clear that engagement is not something that an organization can *do to its workforce.* This is a common misunderstanding, when people ask in Internet forums and elsewhere, *"how can I engage my workforce?"* Instead, management responsibility is to *create an environment that is sufficiently attractive to their workers that those people will choose to engage.* The environment can be physical (lighting, heating, comfort, tools and equipment, etc.) and even more importantly, what we call "psychosocial." The latter means how people are treated, both in formal ways (performance management, etc.) and in the many informal ways in which the relationship between workers and their organizations plays out.

Engagement involves the *emotional component* of feeling good enough about the job and its environment to want to take the *behavioral step* of enthusiastic commitment to the organization's goals and to one's role in the achievement of them. It means that a worker is willing to "go the extra mile," above and beyond simply "doing the job." These are not the people who rush to leave at 5:00 p.m. sharp, even if a customer is calling on the phone! They have subordinated their own needs to a greater degree than those not engaged so that they can support the organization's needs. Clearly though, engaged workers do not do this because it feels bad—there is enjoyment in being engaged, committed to doing something that one is involved in eight or more hours a day. Some (certainly those who complain about their jobs) would say these people are lucky, *but engagement is not luck, it is a conscious choice.*

## In what ways does engagement affect performance?

High engagement organizations have many advantages:

- They are more productive than low engagement peers.
- They are also more profitable, if that is part of their structure.
- Their stock, if listed on exchange(s), performs better than that of low engagement companies.

- Their customers are more satisfied, much more likely to return, and remain loyal.
- Their workers are healthier than those in low engagement, low morale organizations (itself a human and financial cost, as well as a productivity issue).[23]

The previous list is compelling enough for most organizations having sufficiently enlightened leadership to make big efforts in this area, in creating the *high engagement culture*. They know that competitors who have not done so have major disadvantages. Worker engagement is *the* competitive edge. Lack of it imposes major opportunity costs on countries. The MacLeod Report on engagement reported that

> disengaged workers were costing the UK £44 billion per year in lost productivity.[24]

### What drives engagement and disengagement at work?

While we cannot blame the Crash for the low engagement levels, which were in place before it happened, we do see a common mechanism between the Crash and worker engagement, which is central to our theme in this book. *We believe that factors that contributed to the Crash have been present for some time, also eroding morale and engagement.* These will become clear as we examine the different forces that combine to make our workers want to, or not want to, engage at work.

There is no one driver of low worker engagement; like the work culture of which it is part, it is affected by everything from factors within societies as a whole (economic, cultural, etc.), down to those which exist at the organizational level, and further down to the personality of individual people such as CEOs and workers themselves. This is why it can be such a challenge to improve engagement: how do you change the personality of a CEO? As in any complex human behavior such as engagement at work, these are *somewhat* interdependent: how a worker feels at work and *whether she chooses to engage there* is not unconnected from how and where she grew up, in which national culture, etc. Having said this, it does not preclude a multinational organization, with a strong and people-oriented culture and top-quality managers who really live that culture, from having highly engaged workers in many different countries: there are common elements to which most humans respond, no matter where they are. We say "most" humans because of the simple fact that a persistently negative and resistant personality in an individual can override all other positive engagement factors in the same way that one can lead a horse to the water but cannot *make* him drink!

Since culture and engagement are so intertwined, one would expect that factors driving culture also drive engagement. This is exactly what we have found over many surveys around the world. So if we return to our culture pyramid and condense it somewhat so that we can focus on engagement, we then see how things work:

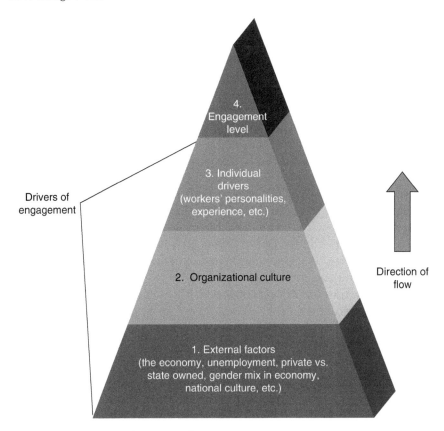

Drivers of engagement

Direction of flow

*Chart 2.2*   From work culture to worker engagement

Since our model shows national culture lower than organizational culture and worker engagement, we are saying that powerful external factors can affect *both* the culture of an organization and the extent to which its workers choose to engage. However we see some external factors having more of an effect on engagement than on the internal culture of many organizations. We will take a look at these now:

**External factors (the economy, unemployment, private vs. state owned, gender mix in economy, etc.)**

*The economy*

The Crash of 2008 is eerily familiar to students of such events, not just in relation to the Great Depression, but more recently to the events that lead to the originally-named "Lost Decade" in Japan (1991–2000). Unfortunately, that lost decade has now been extended by some observers to almost two decades. The scenario, as described in Wikipedia,[25] is remarkable in its resemblance to the Crash of 2008:

> The strong economic growth of the 1980s ended abruptly at the start of the 1990s. In the late 1980s, abnormalities within the Japanese economic system had fueled a massive *wave of speculation by Japanese companies, banks and securities companies.* A combination of exceptionally high land values and *exceptionally low interest rates briefly led to a position in which credit was both easily available and extremely cheap.* This led to massive borrowing, the proceeds of which were invested mostly in domestic and foreign stocks and securities.
>
> Recognizing that this bubble was unsustainable, the Finance Ministry sharply raised interest rates in late 1989. This abruptly terminated the bubble, *leading to a massive Crash in the stock market.* It also led to a debt crisis; a large proportion of the debts that had been run up turned bad, which in turn led to a crisis in the banking sector, with many banks being bailed out by the government.
>
> Michael Schuman of Time Magazine noted that banks kept injecting new funds into unprofitable "zombie firms" to keep them afloat, arguing that they were *too big to fail.* However, most of these companies were too debt-ridden to do much more than *survive on further bailouts,* which led to an economist describing Japan as a "loser's paradise."
>
> (emphasis added)

One of the effects of this period was that the time-honored tradition of lifetime job security for the typical "company man" came to an end. Gone were the days when such a person signed up with a Toshiba or Mitsubishi and stayed there for a whole career. Unlike in the United States with its mobile workforce, much more committed to career and profession than to a particular company, this was considered a highly desirable state of affairs (another example of cultural differences that impact engagement). As a result, engagement dropped like a stone and does not seem to have recovered since, because every survey we have seen has Japan at or near the bottom of worldwide engagement tables.

Outside of Japan, the strikes and other actions such as large-scale demonstrations, which have hit some European countries (the "PIIGS"), and which were detailed in Chapter 1, are a symptom of the major effects on morale and engagement among the large public sector workforces in those countries. The strikes are a direct result of the Crash and its rippling effects around the world: it created a low tide that exposed just how vulnerable may European countries' finances were, especially among some of the more profligate members of the EU. Living beyond their means for decades (a common situation around the world, including in the US), the Crash forced countries to face up to their debts and unsustainable ways, especially their generosity to certain members of their population, working or not. The cutbacks, which have become necessary (and sometimes are enforced by the International Monetary Fund), have spread to affect more than the public sector workers, and have dampened economic growth and thrown millions out of work: the housing market in Spain is a good example. *We can expect significant disengagement of workers in these countries as this painful period plays out.*

While this represents the downward push of poor economic conditions, the positive effect of a good economy on engagement levels is demonstrated very well by the high engagement levels in China and India[26]: here, millions are experiencing improved working conditions and advancement opportunities along with (relative to before) good pay for the first time, many coming into the middle classes as they make the shift from rural to urban living. In China, these changes have come about as economic liberalization has been granted after decades of stultifying communist restraints and turmoil, such as the 1960s Cultural Revolution. We saw this after 1989 when one of us was measuring morale among workers in Europe who had been newly liberated from the Soviet Union: morale in Hungary and Poland and other eastern European locations topped worldwide rankings for quite some time afterwards.

*State versus private ownership*

Trends around the world, from EU countries to Russia, India and China, have been to shed public ownership for private, stockholder or individual owners. This has happened to a greater or lesser extent depending on the country and with some bumps and even some backtracking (Russia, for example) along the road. Some changes have been quite dramatic: to compare pre-Thatcher UK with the present day is to see a whole different landscape, and for one of us who grew up in England, not a day too soon. At one point between World War II and now, steel, telephone, car and truck, coal, rail, and other industries were owned and operated by the UK government. Privatization is driven by regulation: for example, the EU laws ensuring that massive state-owned public companies there would become, at the least, majority private. China stayed a communist country politically but opened up large parts of its economy to private ownership, and the rest is history: liberation of the "tiger economy" has meant rapidly rising standards of living there. We need look no further than the auto industry for a symbolic sign of this rise: in 2010, China overtook the US in terms of car sales.[27] As is the case when people suddenly become free to own and operate their own businesses, or to work in a competitive capitalist economy with rising wages and better working conditions, the levels of morale and engagement hit the roof, as we saw earlier.

This is not to say that publicly owned organizations are doomed to have low levels of worker engagement; indeed they often work as hard to create the conditions necessary for high levels of engagement as anyone in private industry. Since they are limited in how they can compensate people, for example not being able to offer stock options, it is actually very much in their interest that they turn to building the internal culture that will make their workers want to dedicate themselves and "go the extra mile," clear by-products of the engaged workforce. The issue is that engagement and bureaucracy are not good bedfellows, so to the extent that publicly owned organizations can avoid that and behave instead more like the best-run private ones, they can reap the benefits of that with their workforces. If we need any proof that public sector organizations can get it right, we need only look at the military and some police forces, certainly in the US and UK, and most likely elsewhere, where high morale and engagement are not just important, but lives depend on it.

*Case study: Privatization at France Télécom and worker engagement*

One question that emerges from the issue of private versus public ownership goes beyond whether private or public sector workers can and do engage with their organizations; it is whether the *change from one to another (public → private) itself is "disengaging."* The sad and complex case of France Télécom gives us a cautionary example of what can, but does not have to, happen.

In continental Europe the shift from state-owned and -operated to private companies ("privatization") has involved some of the largest companies in that area,[28] including such telecoms as OTE (Greece), Deutsche Telekom (Germany) and France Télécom. This creates major stresses on people, as they have to adapt to private sector working conditions and rules of employment and often, the greater pressure for performance demanded by the profit-oriented private sector. Privatization usually occurs in combination with the opening up of markets, which these companies typically had to themselves as state-owned monopolies. Such competition, as we shall see, undermines profit margins and places enormous pressures on the company to be efficient, pressures it never had to experience before. Of course, this is exactly what the rather Darwinian capitalist system is meant to do, and consumers reap huge benefits from reduced pricing.

In 2009 the news[29] that France Télécom (FT) had suffered the absolute tragedy of multiple suicides of its workers made headlines around the world, and both of us followed the developments with great concern for the company and its people. FT is one the largest telecom companies in the world, with 180,000 employees, of which 100,000 are in France, and international wireless telecom operations known as Orange. Formerly wholly state owned, like most European telecoms, the company had to become majority shareholder owned because of European law, although the French state continues to hold a significant ownership (27%) and can call the shots when it comes to major moves made by the company. When the news emerged that more than 35 people employed by FT had committed suicide in 2008 and 2009, with a further 11 losing their lives in this way in early 2010,[30] some of whom leaving notes indicating *troubles and changes at FT as the reason for their despair*, the French state stepped in with demands for an investigation. This lead to the resignation of the deputy CEO, a former consultant who had been reported as being a hard-charging individual responsible for bringing the company into a more competitive era.

So what happened here? Some early newspaper reports mentioned the fact that France has a fairly high rate of suicide and that with such a large employee population FT's suicides were not out of the ordinary. From a purely cold statistical point of view, this is probably false: teenagers, older people and the unemployed likely have higher suicide rates than those not in those groups, none of whom by definition work for FT, whose suicide rate for employed individuals aged between 19 and 60 might be higher than the French average for that demographic. Having said that, we do not think this statistical approach says enough about the situation, and offers no solution in the case of a finding that FT's actions have indeed contributed to the employees taking their own lives; or to look at it another way, there is a possibility that FT may not have had the high morale that could have prevented these tragedies, regardless of the underlying suicide rate in France. The role of the FT employees themselves must also be considered, not in any negative way of "blaming" them, but from a sympathetic point of view; and we need to look at the role of the French public, FT's customers.

Over the last decade or so, millions and millions of FT's customers have deserted the company, especially younger ones. The advent of services like Skype, which routes calls through the Internet, have devastated old, fixed-line telecoms around the industrialized world. Many young people now would not dream of having a fixed-line phone, but instead rely on their mobile or "handy" and Skype, which gives them free worldwide *audio and video* calling when they are in touch with another Skype user, and extremely cheap calls (around 2 euro cents a minute) when they are not. Clearly FT's cost structure and its staffing levels were created at a time before Skype and other VoIP calling services came along. Internet calling makes this cost structure unsustainable, unless the French public chooses to ignore it and stay with FT's more expensive fixed-line system, which they clearly do not, any more than German consumers have stayed with Deutsche Telekom.

As for the employees' role, let's go back to when a person decided to join France Télécom. Was this a random event? It was not: this person chose to go there based on his or her needs and, especially, values. As we discussed before, this "self selection" normally works well to meet the needs of both the individual worker and the organization.

The problem comes when, for reasons of deregulation or other change in the market environment, the rules of the game change, and the long-established, safe utility is stripped of government ownership or protection, and thrown into a fiercely competitive situation—exactly what happened to France Télécom. Faced with this, the company has to respond with a complete change in its culture and often, with cuts in staffing levels to meet the cost structure of its newfound competition. Those who thought they were "safe" at the company until retirement suddenly find out that they are as vulnerable as those who joined very different industries when they entered the workforce.[31] *Depending on how this is managed*, it can cause almost unbearable stress, *even when workers still have many built-in protections, as mentioned in our note 31.* Often, just the fear created by such a big change is enough to create the high stress levels FT experienced. Of course, this is not their fault, things changed around them; at the same time, change is everywhere at all times, and the idea that we can stop the clock and "keep things as they are" is impossible in life.

This is not to say that resistance, failure or inability to adapt are universal in this situation: there are those who will thrive in a new competitive environment and enjoy the new challenges. They might even experience a sense of freedom from the old way of doing things and the rigidities of that style of management that often comes with government-run or heavily regulated utilities. They might enjoy the opportunities that open up to them. This happened in many of the US utilities, which have been deregulated over the last decades. Other employees will not respond so favorably, they will not make it and the stress level will build up to intense levels. They simply cannot let go of what they thought was lifetime job security and safety and a certain work lifestyle—witness Japan and the "lost decades" of the 1990s and 2000s, which we discussed earlier.

The key is that the company going through this wrenching change has to be sensitive to employee needs and have an understanding and a plan to deal with what we have described previously, and some do not. This is also about corporate values, and about morale: some of our former clients have also gone through huge change and (while significantly smaller, which does not have to be the main issue) avoided the tragic outcome of FT; they did this by having a strong culture of "putting people first," not as an empty slogan but as a living, breathing part of their culture. This was communicated and trained relentlessly and lived in the organization without exception. Their organizational morale was constantly improving, which "inoculated" them against the worst, most negative outcomes of change. If a cut in staffing levels seemed necessary, for example, they bent over backwards to ease the pain by cutting work hours for all, rather than individuals. We have no inside information on FT, but it seems that with the new and widespread intervention, the company will have the opportunity to focus on these issues in a way that they did not do before. It is not the employees' fault that such wrenching change happens; at the same time, neither the government nor an individual company can protect everyone from change, such as the Skype example, any more than King Canute could stop the tide from coming in on the English shoreline. It is how we help people understand it and adapt to it, how we build the high morale and engagement culture that can cushion its worst effects, that is important, and we ignore this at our—and the employees'—peril.

*Gender mix in economy, paternalism and the role of women*

As it turns out, the economies that are seeing more and more women entering the workforce are reaping a huge advantage: not only are they providing this freedom and opportunity to contribute to half their population, but they may be increasing engagement at work! The US provides an excellent example of this: some 60% of women work, and almost 50% of jobs in the US economy are now held by women. Amazingly, women now occupy the *majority* of professional and managerial jobs. It is likely that this trend will accelerate, as American women now go to college more than men, and college degrees have a huge effect on job prospects and earnings. Women are now the primary breadwinners in 40% of US households and hold the majority of jobs in the five fields expected to grow the most in the next decade.[32]

The connection to engagement comes via a 2007 study by David Gaddis Ross, a Professor at Columbia Business School in New York. He studied the effect of having women at senior levels of management in 2000 of the largest US organizations, and found that firms with more women at those levels were more profitable. His summary of the findings indicated that *well-known engagement drivers were the cause of this*:

> Overall, the data suggest that firms that promote women to senior management positions enjoy economically superior performance because of the *complementary set of interpersonal management skills related to inclusiveness and the encouragement of employee voices that women bring to the table.*[33]

> (emphasis added)

On an NBC News report related to women at work, Professor Ross expanded on this theme by emphasizing the fact that women are *more democratic in their management style, more collaborative and less dictatorial.*[34] It is not a major leap to suggest that, as a result of these powerful engagement drivers, and knowing what we do about engagement being itself a driver of profitability, the female effect in senior jobs could be very favorable. Whether the fact of women occupying senior positions *is responsible alone for superior profitability* or merely a correlation is not entirely clear, even though Professor Ross seems to have examined this data for the correlation-causation question. Perhaps there is a common third element in companies that hire women as senior executives and the fact that they are profitable. This certainly requires more investigation, but if confirmed, it sets the stage for improvements in engagement brought about by a national trend, and bodes very well indeed for the expansion of women's participation in work in organizations in general and management in particular.[35]

Continuing on the role of women at work, but from a different angle, let's imagine a paternalistic culture somewhere in the world. There are plenty of examples so we do not need to single one out. What effect does this paternalism have on organizations? More than likely, it will have a big effect. For one thing most managers, especially top managers, will by definition be men. Secondly, those men will have a certain attitude we could summarize as "Father Knows Best." This creates an organizational culture that is based on top-down management, authoritarianism, control and very little real workplace democracy. Of course, such men do not have to be brutal, they can be quite paternalistically kind; but the possibilities for women in these societies and their organizations are limited, sometimes severely so. If women do work outside the home, they often have little chance to advance, to learn and to grow. In such situations, the idea of "engagement" for women at work is an unattainable luxury; it is also limited for men, even though they appear to be the beneficiaries of the system. This is because a system that keeps women down ultimately keeps everyone down.

This is not our imagination. We have seen it in effect around the world, and any employee survey worth its salt will flash a red alert when it comes to this kind of management style. Across the list of engagement drivers that have to do with opportunity, advancement, being heard, delegation and so on, the paternalistic boss does very badly indeed, even among men.

We are not just talking about Third World or emerging countries here: even some "sophisticated" European and other societies suffer somewhat from this affliction. For example, despite being plugged into larger trading and political networks such as the EU (and inevitably being influenced by countries in that network, which are much different in terms of women), some countries still seem to hang on to their long-entrenched paternalistic ways. It will take more time before they wake up to the positive benefits of women in the workplace and the pro-engagement management styles they bring with them.

*National culture*[36]

Gender mix and paternalism are only part of the cultural bedrock on which organizations are built and which affect how they operate and how/whether workers engage with their workplaces. Other aspects of national cultures come into to play as far as this is concerned. What is interesting in the national culture-worker engagement equation is that sometimes culture can be the only reason why we find what might otherwise seem to be incongruent data in the area of worker engagement. This is the case with Germany.

*Case study: Germany, engagement and national culture*

One of us lives part time in Germany, has consulted there for a long period and has therefore had a chance to observe it up close. The net result of this is a deep respect for the country and its hardworking and interesting people. German products are in huge demand around the world, and as we write this, Germany has been experiencing a post-Crash mini-boom, coupled with lower unemployment, as exports to Asia pick up.[37]

The experience of a long time spent in another country, combined with a not insignificant amount of data collected from some of its organizations in the area of worker morale and engagement, is a good basis for observations, but does not by itself answer the big question: *why are German workers so disengaged?*

Gallup reports that the percentage of German workers they consider to be engaged, as measured by a representative national sample of people polled with the widely used Q12 Gallup engagement questionnaire, has hovered around 13% for some years. Our readers with good memories will recall that this compares to a still low 29% for the United States. How can Germany be so low, even during times not considered economically so bad? Are wages so low? No, they are among the highest in the industrialized world. Are there pitifully short vacations? No, Germans are among the most vacationed workers in the world, with average vacation periods of up to six weeks per year. So what is the problem here? *It must come down to one thing: management.*

No, we are not going to jump into overused stereotypes here and condemn the entire management sector of German business. Clearly, they must be doing a lot of things right to be in such a commanding position with so many of their products worldwide. What we are going to do is suggest that the culture of that society *does* have an impact on management styles. This is not just our opinion, but is also that of the *Gallup Management Journal*, where the engagement data are to be found.[38] They begin by discussing the enormous costs of a disengaged workforce:

> Gallup estimates that actively disengaged employees cost the German economy between 81.2 billion and 109 billion euros per year in lost productivity alone. This does not include additional costs to the economy due to absenteeism, lack of innovation and customer orientation, high turnover, and negative word-of-mouth.[39]

In question after question on the Q12, such as customer orientation, advocacy,[40] willingness to remain employed with their current employer or whether they have had recent positive feedback from their boss, German workers who are engaged *score far above those who are not*. So German companies know from this data what works and in which direction they must change to create the conditions for greater engagement of their workforce. But seemingly, not many do this, and this is where the culture comes in. As Gallup says:

> The problem in Germany is largely "homemade" and can be attributed to a lack of good leadership ... The typical German approach to management relies *on seniority rather than merit*. Traditionally, the role of the supervisor is hierarchical—56% of workers describe their supervisor's behavior as top-down, while 44% say their supervisor manages "like a team member." Rigid social formalities[41] are the rule.[42]

(emphasis added)

Nothing demonstrates the differences in culture-driving management practices and worker behavior as well as a side-by-side comparison of businesses in the same industry, but based in different cultures. *When those businesses are owned by the same company, the comparison is even more powerful.* This is exactly what we have with Aldi and Trader Joe's, which are two arms of the same company, the famous Aldi food store chain from Germany.

Aldi (the word Aldi means "Albrecht Discount" because it was created by the Albrecht brothers, who became billionaires as a result of their creation) is a wildly successful concept for the German food market, selling a limited selection of inexpensive and good quality items in a fast-paced environment, which flushes customers one way through the aisles rather like IKEA. When one reaches checkout, the real fun begins, not only when a lane opens, which creates a stampede, but also when one reaches the clerk doing the scanning. Let us just say, you had better be prepared! Get your bag(s) ready, and fill them as soon as you can. You will receive no help from anyone to load your shopping, and heaven help you if you load slowly and drag out the waiting time for the line—the withering looks you get will drive you to a higher-end store like Tengelmann next time, if you are thin skinned.

Now let's cross the Atlantic to the US, where Aldi owns a food store chain with a remarkably different culture, Trader Joe's. TJ's, as it is called by its many fans, was bought by Aldi around 1979, but few if any Americans know that. TJ's and Aldi's German stores could not be more different, not so much in the way they look or the quality of food they sell, although that is a bit different, but in the way things work. At TJ's a line that opens does not result in a stampede, instead the person first in a longer line will be invited to be first in the new one. On arriving at the checkout, clerks will, in a remarkably relaxed and friendly way, check your stuff then load it expertly into the bag(s). No rush, no frenetic feeling, yet it all happens fast. TJ's does not necessarily have more customers in the store at one time than Aldi, and yet it will always have six or so checkout lines going. Aldi tops out at three and often has only one, with the line snaking back into the store. That changes when enough people call out, *neue Kasse*, or as the military would say, "call for backup!"

How is this possible? Clearly TJ's is a profitable enterprise even given the apparent inefficiencies built into the system vis-à-vis its parent's German stores, such as more checkout clerks and loading of customers' bags by them. We would bet that Aldi has studied the numbers and would introduce the German system if they could, but of course they can't! This is because the US has a shopping and general service culture, which demands that customers be treated in a certain way. Having to stuff your own bags would be seen as a major insult; having the clerks do that is a minimum expectation. Having long checkout lines, the same. Germans are of course rather more oriented to rules than "unruly" Americans and perhaps they see the Aldi system as "those are the rules and I abide by them." Faced with this situation, Americans would say, "those are the rules and unless they change I am voting with my feet and going elsewhere."

This is a book about worker engagement and here is where we are leading to: one of us has shopped Aldi in Germany many times and when we look at the workers there they look *somewhat burned out* and certainly harried, tired and stressed. They rush from one task to another as if their life depended on it, and that includes when they have checkout duty. On a recent visit to a German Aldi, a friend of ours was looking for an item she could not find and a clerk who was stocking shelves was working in the area; instead of stopping to help our friend, the clerk berated her for being in the way! The pressure on the clerks seems to be so intense that stopping for a customer seems like almost the last thing they want to do.

Trader Joe's people on the other hand, no matter what state they are in, seem to have that "laid back" relaxed style even though they work fast and efficiently. They are friendly. We are willing to bet their morale and engagement is head and shoulders above that of their German colleagues, which has many significant long-term implications for their business, their longevity on the job and, yes, on their individual health. This is a shame. Aldi has proved that they can master a system in the US that makes both workers and customers happy. For one of us as an Aldi customer in Germany, we only tolerate it to get the cheap coffee, cheese and wine, which they have. No cheaper than Trader Joe's, though.

When we posted this information on a blog, a European with experience in northern cultures on that continent responded:

I think it has to do with the perception of the customers. In Germany, Belgium, the Netherlands or even France we are not used to so much customer service. We perceive it as fake and over acting. Not necessary. At the same time (in Europe) Aldi isn't known for their customer service or happy shopping experiences. You go to Aldi to buy cheap groceries. If you would like more services you go to another store/chain.[43]

In other words, it's the culture, this is what we expect and why we do not demand more; it is also a trade-off we are willing to make. Beyond this, however, is the question of engagement, and its effect on the workers, their health and so on. If a grocery chain can be run with high engagement *by the same company* in one country, can it not be run like that in another, even if that goes against the grain of that culture to a degree? If only to gain the benefits—for everyone involved, workers and customers—which would accrue? Imagine if more German companies did this, the 13% German engagement level would rise and Germany would become unstoppable given its current success levels, which it achieves even with low engagement.

### Social class

As we saw earlier, HayGroup has stated that the UK has one of the lowest worker engagement levels in Europe. Can this be attributed to cultural factors such as social class? Or is lack of management skill to blame for this? Clearly, class factors can have a great impact on how a country's business culture functions. To suggest otherwise would be to ignore history: in 1789 France embarked on its revolution and executed some 2000 aristocrats, while monarchs around Europe looked on with some trepidation. When the French Republic emerged, it made sure that the extreme social inequalities of its pre-revolutionary period would not be repeated, and French culture still adheres strongly to those beliefs. Do not expect to hear "my name is Pierre and I will be your waiter today!" (combined with a big smile)—or even be treated in a moderately "service oriented" way—by most Parisian waiters! This is exactly the "fake" aspect of American service that Europeans so despise and is seen in France as a prime example of inequality. Those days ended when heads rolled in what is now the *Place de la Concorde*. For the same reasons, one does not expect extremes in other conditions at work, such as pay, in France. Liberty, *Equality* and Fraternity rule the way they do things.

The UK is a different story though; having never gone though a revolution, its monarchy and aristocracy survived, even if the latter was beaten down somewhat by successive Labour governments' inheritance tax policies. Partly as a result of never having followed the French lead and gone through a revolution, the UK follows more of the US model of *laissez-faire* capitalism. Its social class structure has also remained somewhat in place, with trainee doctors and lawyers still emerging much more from the (socioeconomic) "upper classes" than the "lower" in 2004, in roughly the same percentages as they did some eight or more years earlier, especially in medicine.[44] Is this the reason for low engagement in the UK: that there is lack of opportunity in these and other "high end" professions, or upward mobility for workers, because of their class background? Or does management treat "lower class" workers in some condescending way because of their socioeconomic background? We cannot definitely answer these questions but pose them merely to demonstrate the many cultural factors that work together to determine whether workers in a particular country are engaged or not.

### Globalization, political changes and the push for democracy

Several national and societal issues are therefore present as drivers or limiters of engagement at work; while some of these are based on long held "traditions" or customs in these countries, they are not as static as one might imagine, because of the increasingly rapid changes in the world. Two of the main pressures to shift are the effects of *globalization* and the heated competition this brings to *worldwide trade*. This creates a need for efficiency and productivity, *both of which are heavily influenced by worker engagement*. But there is much more to it than this, because we can never underestimate the push for humanity to evolve in the direction of freedom and democracy; recent events in Egypt, Tunisia and Libya provide a spectacular demonstration of this. With political democracy comes the push for democracy at work—they are in lockstep, *and that can lead to greater worker engagement*. As the dictator falls so do the mini-dictators in workplaces throughout those newly freed countries, which made themselves in the image of the "leader," and were able to get away with it as long as this model operated. But when democracy rears its powerful head, all this changes—sometimes overnight.

With or without seismic political shifts such as this, though, which country can afford to hold onto practices that leave its workers disengaged and demotivated? Which people around the world want to live like this? In the more successful parts of the developing world, the push from workers to be treated better and to be able to contribute more of their skills and talents will increase, as living standards rise from mere subsistence to middle class and beyond.

While these events involving globalization and increased political freedom play out across the world, societies are being forced to change, to adapt, in order to meet the needs of their people and to be competitive.

> The engagement of each country's workers with the organizations where they work will become an essential element determining whether that country can compete in this new world: *other things being equal, those countries which can find a way to create the conditions for high worker engagement will have a major competitive edge.*

At the *organizational level*, this will have profound consequences, since many of the most significant drivers of worker engagement reside there. The pressures to improve the "way we do things" will only increase.

## Organizational culture

We have taken an extensive trip through the external factors driving part of the worker engagement levels, which we see around the world. The reason for this is that

- External factors over which we have little or no direct control do have an impact on worker engagement; we wanted to fully explore these now to make their effects clear. However, our focus from here on will only be on the things we can control and change.
- We want to make clear that 100% control of a "high-engagement environment" is not always possible, even under ideal circumstances, and that there will always be something "on the outside" having an impact.

However, this is never the reason to make an excuse and give up, because even in places where there is unemployment, or a particular national culture that is perhaps more rigid, there are organizations that enjoy the benefits of a highly engaged workforce! They have found a way to be mindful of external factors, but work around them, or mitigate them. We have worked in inner-city US hospitals where external conditions were dreadful, and yet the staff inside the hospitals dealt with these conditions heroically and with a high level of engagement. We have seen it demonstrated time and again that such things are possible, no matter the circumstances. This brings us to the influence of the organization's culture on engagement, since our examples of "winning against all odds" were driven by exactly that: they knew how to treat people and how to create that environment internally that was so attractive and rewarding for their workers. It is these practices we will detail in Chapter 4. First though we need to be mindful of what happens when a particular internal culture, even a great one, meets people: *it doesn't always "work."*

## Individual drivers

### Personality and clinical disorders

Since engagement at work is a *behavior involving choice*, we cannot ignore the individual differences that exist in people who choose to engage and those who do not. Imagine a perfect place to work, in terms of everything we have described as necessary in the physical and "psychosocial" environment. The list of everything one might want in a good job is there:

- The organization's goals are clear and well communicated.
- The organization's mission is one that adds to society's well-being.

- The culture is open and communicative.
- The physical environment is pleasant.
- Managers are supportive and focused on helping people succeed.
- Pay is competitive externally and fair internally.
- Opportunities for advancement exist and are filled fairly.
- The organization is successful in its marketplace and likely to be around for quite some time and to grow.
- It has a good image with customers and with its local community.

It sounds like paradise, doesn't it? Yet if we surveyed the workers there, no matter how well everyone had been selected (and such organizations normally do a good job of hiring, along with everything else), we would find some disgruntled people. Why is this?

- They might just be having a "bad day."
- They might have a lot of stress in their personal lives right now.
- They might have had a bad experience with a client or a sale that fell through.

These things are all normal and pass with (hopefully a short period of) time, but they do not cover everyone. Other situations are much more worrying:

- They might be difficult most of the time.
- They might complain a lot, not only to co-workers but even to customers.
- They might get into fights with co-workers.
- They might hold on to things that happen in the normal course of work life, bear grudges, and never let them go and move on.
- They might be very resistant to management, and "hard to handle."
- They might blame others for just about everything that happens and never take personal responsibility.

Such people can be very toxic to a work environment and invariably take up far more management attention than one wishes to spend on any one individual. Sometimes we meet them in focus groups, where they might try (unsuccessfully) to dominate the time with their endless complaints and perceived grievances. Worse, these traits do not always appear at the initial interview(s), which is why multiple interviews are always a good idea, including with the team with whom they will work or the one they will manage. Underlying reasons can have to do with "personality" issues[45] or in more extreme cases be part of clinically diagnosable afflictions such as *Borderline Personality Disorder*. Engagement is a choice, *and not everyone is capable of making it, no matter how great the environment.* This is why probationary periods are used by so many organizations. It is also why so many organizations use some kind of personality test such as the MMPI[46] or similar, to find out more about the person they are about to employ than that person is willing, or able, to tell them directly. *Knowing who will and who won't be able and willing to engage is the reason why great recruiters*, and managers who are smart about recruiting, are nearly always in high demand.

## Top management and Boards of directors

All of this means very little if top management and Boards of directors are not 100% on board with engagement efforts. If that is the case, it is often because they have a resistance to any such activity in the first place and find it too "soft," or because they have illusions about how things are in their organizations. Recent research illustrates that the latter is certainly something we are up against in the drive to enhance engagement. It is well illustrated in a 2010 study in Europe and the Middle East by HayGroup and the Economist Intelligence Unit (EIU).[47] Some 331 executives were surveyed, of which about half were C-suite or Board level. What they said tells us that, no matter how much the drumbeat of engagement gets louder, and activities like worker surveys are more widespread, some at the very top of our organizations have a very different view of "reality" than the people who work for them at other levels in the organization:

- Of the C-suite executives, 65% say their main method of engaging is company-wide communications about strategy.
  - Only 26% say "ensuring mid managers are capable of good people management."
  - *Only 23% mention anything about philosophy and organization culture.*
- More than half of C-suite executives believe that they themselves have been the biggest determinant (driver) of levels of engagement in the organization, but only one in six director level managers agree with that! *Not one C-suite executive mentioned HR as the driver of engagement levels in their organization.*
- Some 63% of "C-suiters" think that their organization has much higher or higher engagement levels than the competition; but 56% of directors disagree!
- Although 84% of respondents say that disengaged workers are one of the biggest threats to their business

    only 12% of respondents report that their companies "regularly and often" tackle staff with "continually low engagement". Even according to C-suite executives alone, engagement is discussed "occasionally", "rarely" or "never" at board level in 43% of companies.[48]

- Shockingly, to us at least, *fewer than one in seven among the C-suite believe that middle managers or line managers are "chiefly responsible"* for employee engagement in their organization.
  - o This goes against all the research we have seen and published about the true axis of engagement in organizations. Moreover, if these managers sense that they are not held accountable by their own bosses on this issue, it stands to reason that many of them will not break their necks trying to boost engagement.

With attitudes such as this and the yawning gap between those at the top and just the next level "down," no wonder some organizations languish at the lower reaches of the engagement levels. Some countries too, as we will now see.

## How was worker engagement before the crash, and how is it now?

First, a brief primer on engagement, morale and job satisfaction: we have already defined engagement and morale and hope that we have clearly conveyed the idea that they are related but different in terms of their psychological state (behavior versus state of mind). Job satisfaction is also used widely as a measure of "how things are" at work and since a lot of data is collected around the world on that topic, we cannot ignore its existence when we look at trends. There are four issues:

- Job satisfaction is sometimes used to mean "level of morale" even though, strictly speaking, it is much more limited. One should always be mindful of this when looking at such data.
- In the strictest sense of the phrase and usage, job satisfaction is simply that: it is a worker satisfied with his or her job? In many cases, no other data is collected that would clarify why that person does or does not like the job. Often this topic is measured with a single question, further showing the very limited focus.[49]
- Nonetheless, job satisfaction has been shown, even in some robust studies, to be a powerful measure of a more general sense of well-being, and a strong predictor of engagement *and performance.*[50]
- If we therefore use some data here on job satisfaction, it might seem to be outside the area of engagement, which is our focus here, but in fact it is not.

So if we could do an MRI or CAT-scan image of a typical organization in Europe or the US right now, what would we see? How would we find levels of worker engagement and morale as we deal, still, with the after-effects of the Crash?

How were those levels *before* the Crash? (In other words, if we fell, was it from a high level, or not?) How would this differ from places where the Crash was barely felt? What would we see as the other organizational after-effects of the Crash? What are the implications of all this?

### Engagement before the Crash

Worker engagement before the Crash was not especially good in the US, most European and some Asian countries: *it was average at best and in some cases well below worldwide averages.* To fall still further from that level would therefore be a worrisome situation. International management consultant Mercer reported in 2008 some worldwide engagement trends, which put things into perspective: their research pointed out that while emerging dynamos Brazil, India and China (three-quarters of the so-called BRIC cohort) lead the world in this area, many Western countries such as France, Germany and Portugal were well below average; at the bottom of the list were Japan and South Korea, while the US was barely edging above worldwide averages.[51]

### Engagement, morale and job satisfaction trends in selected worldwide locations

The idea that the Crash had an effect on worker engagement would seem to be a "no brainer." However, it is controversial, as this blog post[52] discusses in detail; some of the controversy relates to how engagement is defined and measured. While several large survey research firms show downward trends of some significance, Gallup shows something quite counter-intuitive: that US engagement has been flat for most of the period of the Crash (*see the quote ahead*). How can this be? For one thing, engagement surveys are carried out with those who are employed. The eight million people who lost their jobs in the US after the Crash are clearly not surveyed for engagement. However, even workers who remained after job cuts would have been expected to be fearful that they would be next, and would that not affect their morale and engagement levels? We have talked elsewhere about those who survive layoffs; they are sometimes so glad to have "survived" that that feeling mitigates the downward pressure on morale and engagement caused by the lingering fear that they might have lost their jobs and still could, in the future.[53]

Gallup is not, however, the only game in town when it comes to engagement trends worldwide. It is helpful to look at not only their data but also that of many other research houses in this area. What do the detailed results tell us? The 2009/2010 U.S. Strategic Rewards Study from Watson Wyatt and World at Work[54] found that US employee engagement levels for all workers at the companies surveyed had *dropped by nearly 10%* between the Crash (September 2008) and one year later.

In contrast, Jennifer Robison wrote in the *Gallup Management Journal* (as reprinted in The Free Library)[55] on January 14, 2010 (well into the recession) that

> Gallup has tracked the engagement levels of the U.S. working population for the past decade. Its most recent employee engagement research shows that *28% of American workers are engaged*, 54% are not engaged, and 18% are actively disengaged ... In addition, from July 2008 to March 2009—during the heart of the recession—Gallup tracked a large sample of employees and found only slight (1%) changes in overall engagement. *In July 2008, 31% of employees were engaged*, 51% were not engaged, and 17% were actively disengaged. *In March 2009, these percentages had changed very minimally: 30% were engaged*, 52% were not engaged, and 18% were actively disengaged.
>
> (emphasis added)

Outside the US, Mercer reports that in the UK: "Employees' levels of engagement are much lower than they were pre-recession, with levels of commitment to the organisation dropping by 17 percentage points since 2006."[56]

Management consultant HayGroup[57] reported in late 2010 a rather shocking series of results, in relation to UK engagement levels, from surveys carried out around the world. Their conclusions were that

- UK workers are the least engaged among major Western European countries.
- Almost a quarter of staff were described as "ineffective" by managers.
- Eighty two percent of UK senior managers (C-Suite executives) regarded disengaged employees as *one of the three greatest threats facing their business*.[58]

(emphasis added)

Germany is an interesting case, which we discussed when looking at national culture and its effects on engagement, and at the contrast between Aldi's German and US (Trader Joe's) food stores. If we look at their national engagement data in more detail, we see that Gallup reported months after the Crash that workers in Germany have *extraordinarily low levels of engagement, even compared to low US levels*. Historical trends are of no comfort: *only 13–16% of German workers were seen by Gallup as having been engaged at work, with the higher numbers (16%) not seen since 2001–2002*.[59] Since Germany has been on a mini-boom as we write this book, due to exports to emerging giants in Asia, we expect that levels might have improved; working against this is the fact that engagement levels *were so very low, for such a long period, even before the Crash*. All is not lost, however. Later we will see that underneath the averages are positive success stories: we will show that one big German company, BMW, is moving in a positive direction and how they are doing it.

While using a different scale and generating different data, the Kenexa Research Institute had similar findings, as far as leaders (India) and laggards (Japan) in worldwide engagement, as of late 2010.[60]

International management consultant TowersWatson produces a Global Workforce Report[61] every few years, and did so in 2010. This is based on a survey of some 22,000 individuals, conducted via the Internet, in 22 worldwide markets. Towers' findings are worth examining for their insight both globally and for some individual countries. Globally, they demonstrate just how much the Crash and resulting recession has affected workers' *sense of security*, and how they feel about leadership and mid-level management:

> The desire for security and stability trumps everything else right now, in part because employees see security as a fast-disappearing part of the deal ... Confidence in leaders and managers is disturbingly low—particularly in terms of the interpersonal aspects of their respective roles.[62]

While there is a need for security, however, the recession has had a marked effect, which surely undermines that need among the global workforce: it has changed the "social contract" between worker and organization and created a much more conditional future out of a guaranteed one. To survive this, *workers will have to become much more self-reliant.* Towers' data supports a thesis we have already introduced and will increasingly develop:

> *"business as usual" on the people front is not an option because there is no business as usual any more.*[63]

That part of the Towers Global Workforce Report that deals with the UK[64] also yields up valuable information related to worker engagement:

> [O]ver half of disengaged [UK] employees are not making plans to leave their current employer. These high levels of *"retained but disengaged"* staff poses a risk [sic] to UK businesses as the economy begins the long road to recovery. As if to underline the risk still further, the Study finds that *key talent, such as high potential employees, are far more likely to move jobs if opportunities arise.*
> (emphasis added)

When asked by Towers what they look for in senior leadership, 71% of UK workers said, "Be trustworthy;" 63% said, "Care about the well being of others;" and 56% said, "Be highly visible to employees." On the other end of the scale, only 22% said "Promote brand/image of the organization." In other words, they are saying, *"Please do what it takes to create the conditions where we want to, and can, engage!"*

Of significant interest to this discussion is the finding made by the world's largest human resource professional organization (with 250,000 members), the *Society for Human Resource Management (SHRM)*. As they reported in their *2011 Trendbook*,[65] when US HR leaders were asked what effects the Crash and resulting recession had on their organization, *morale was picked as second only to the (in)ability to maintain headcount in terms of negative impact, and even higher than financial impact: in fact, 80% of respondents said that the Crash had had a "large or somewhat negative impact" on morale in their organization.*

Whichever source of data we examine, then, it is clear that

- While *changes in engagement levels* in the US from pre- to post-Crash are the subjects of some controversy, pre-Crash levels of engagement there were low (28–31% engaged) and, according to one source (Gallup), have stayed low since then. Other sources say that job satisfaction and engagement in the US have dropped considerably post-Crash.
- Engagement levels are very low in Germany (13% engaged),[66] France, the UK and especially in Japan and South Korea.
- They have gone down in the UK and many other countries, even among those who escaped with their jobs intact during the Great Recession.
- Large-scale organizations with their finger on the pulse of people issues in organizations worldwide, such as SHRM, have leadership survey data showing that morale has been negatively affected by the Crash, *even more so than financial results.*
- At least in the UK and probably elsewhere, organizational leadership is extremely concerned about this state of affairs.

This data is hardly reassuring, showing as it does the low levels of engagement in several major countries and the extent to which engagement was already low before, and has sunk further during and since the Crash. In order to improve from these levels, which bring with them many negative implications for the performance of our organizations, we need to examine the reasons why they are so low in the first place.

## Conclusions

Work culture and worker engagement are a core part of the makeup of those places where we spend so much of our lives, and ultimately determine much of how we feel at work and whether we and our organizations are successful. Inevitably national cultures have an impact, as we have seen, but this is less and less as globalization creates the situation where our organizations straddle the boundaries between countries. India-born managers show up in the UK as they do in the US, and bring their fresh ideas and experiences with them.

Young US and British workers go to Bangalore for a unique experience and the invaluable learning that occurs when one leaves one's own culture. Chinese companies and their managers are showing up around the world, like their Japanese counterparts did decades ago, as China extends its influence. We all learn from each other, and find out that no one *national* culture has all the answers when it comes to *organizational* culture and engagement.

What we do know is that all work cultures are not created equal: we see the Apples, Googles, Virgins, Tata Motors and others, and know that they have something special, which goes beyond engineering or finance or strategy. They have a culture that *produces and sustains* that great engineering and marketing and customer service and makes their people excited to work there and to contribute.

Worker engagement is no simple topic, involving as it does the rich mosaic of contributing factors we have examined. Some of these can be controlled (whom we hire or promote, the culture we create inside our organizations), others we can only work with, react to and mitigate (the economy, national cultures, etc.). But even in reactive mode such as during the 2008 Crash we have choices, some of which will themselves be creators of favorable environments for engagement, and some will not. As we have seen, most countries not in the emerging areas of Asia have their work cut out for them, in regard to worker engagement. Levels of engagement are not especially high across large areas of the developed world, and many have slipped as the effects of the Crash played out; we have also seen why this is so important, in terms of lost productivity and competitiveness. This is hardly the time to be slipping, as competition heats up to unprecedented levels.

While we have covered the drivers of work culture and engagement in some detail as we moved from national to organization to individual levels, we have only hinted at one of the most significant ones, playing its role relentlessly and often outside of many peoples' conscious awareness. It occupies a unique space in that it can clearly be said to have *played a role in both the Crash, and in ongoing low worker engagement around the world.* It is the *ego.*

# 3
# Ego at Work: The Common Thread between the Crash and Low Engagement

In discussing the causes of the Crash and those that lead to low engagement among workers, we have deliberately left out what we believe to be the elephant in the room, *the common thread that runs between them, the ego*. This is such a big subject, and one that is not covered frequently enough as a driver of all kinds of things at work, none of them good. Just like the unfortunate people who embody too much of this particular trait, the ego deserves special attention!

We all know ego when we see it. If you were a film-goer in 1988 and saw *Beaches* with Bette Midler, you might remember a classic line where, after going on and on about herself, she suddenly stops, and says words to the effect that that is certainly enough about "me," now let's hear what the rest of you think about me!

Let's look into this mischievous character trait now in much more detail.

## What is the ego?

Ego: it is such a small word, and yet one that carries a lot of weight. Ego affects most relationships, to some degree, including those at work. In several ways, *ego acts like a psychological virus*:

- Ego requires a human host, which it "infects."
- Ego in excess can be deadly for its human host.
- Even when not deadly, it can and does degrade human life and drain it of many of its joys.
- It is able to hide so that its host has no idea that he/she is "infected."
- When discovered, ego can mutate so that it is once again hidden.
- Ego makes its host defend it and ensure its continued existence, even when that is against the host's best interest.
- Ego has a deep "bag of tricks" to stay invisible, and to maintain itself.

55

- Like with a virus, cases can be very mild and almost symptom-free or severe and life-threatening.

So ego and a virus have a lot in common, including the fact that ego inhabits a human "host," to a greater or lesser extent. Nearly everyone seems to have one, judging by just looking at the world, but some members of the spiritual and religious community strive to, and say they achieve, an ego-free existence.[1] Whether that is just their ego talking is a delightfully circular question we cannot answer here, but we give *some of them* the benefit of the doubt! For the others, we are more cautious: when one of us lived for an 18-month period on the Hawaiian island of Maui about ten years ago, it was not uncommon to hear people brag about how they were more spiritually advanced, more enlightened, than others. We waited with baited breath to hear the ultimate egoistic self-congratulation, *"my ego is smaller than yours,"* but never actually did. But the tricky ego was at work all the time, exactly as Tolle describes in his book detailed further.

Ego for Freudian psychologists is a relatively benign "self" that controls and moderates the impulses coming up from deep inside, from a place they call the "id," *but we will not be using it that way.* Instead we will focus on its everyday conversational use:

> If we look at the dictionary definitions of *ego*, there is quite a range.[2] They start with the simple "I" but then move into the more negative connotations such as "conceit" and "self-importance." Derived from the Latin for "I," ego is generally used in conversation in a different sense than simply that, and in most cases means a separate *part* of "me." It is not just any part, though, ego is an *inflated* "me" (as in "egotist"), which usually *believes itself to be better than others.*

The Princeton University WordNet online dictionary brings all this into focus with a concise definition very aligned with how most people see and use the word "ego":

An inflated feeling of pride in your superiority to others.[3]

We believe the range of definitions, from simple "I" to something far less benign, usefully reflects how the ego develops in human beings:

- At birth and for some time thereafter we seem to feel quite at one with the world, but then inevitably a separate ego or "me" emerges, which for many people (once they get past the "terrible twos"!) will remain a relatively small part of their life from then on. That is, their behavior will be tempered by consideration for others.

- At first, it is a separate sense of self, no more than "me," separate from "you." This in turn takes on a sense of ownership as in "mine and not yours." With *time and the right circumstances*, however, ego can become invested with much more, some of it with very negative outcomes for its "host."
- Whether the ego completely takes over its host or merely stays benignly in the background is partly determined by *how separate that person experiences themselves from others. This separation* is therefore a key component of ego to which we will return again and again; for most it is experienced at a modest level, while for some it will be more extreme.
- *Ego and separation* have a codependency in that the more separation, the more the ego can develop, and the more ego develops, the more that person becomes separate from others.[4]
- In addition to separation, ego can develop into something more toxic when the individual senses themselves to be "less than" as a result of some emotional trauma in the environment, such as rejection.
- Ego's ability to take over its human "host" is also very much determined by *how much reinforcement it can collect from outside the individual*. A person aware of this aspect of themselves (*which is not someone totally in its grip*) might say: "*Don't give me too many compliments, it will inflate my EGO!*"
- Severe cases of ego possession result in the host losing their original "true" identity and leading a life purely driven by the needs and identity of the ego. Coming back from this state can be a painful and difficult journey as the individual struggles to regain their real sense of self while uncovering and letting go of the false ego-based persona[5] they have built over the years.

The ego's need for reinforcement significantly affects others in a relationship with a heavily ego-driven individual, whether a boss, a co-worker or a spouse, *who feel a constant pressure to fulfill that person's ego-driven needs.*

In general the ego builds and reinforces itself through a *process of identification*, whereby its host (us) becomes "better than" others by being identified with objects, people, events, education, achievement, even the brand name stenciled on a T-shirt or woven onto a pair of jeans. In severe cases of ego-possession, the "real" person inside is far less visible or available than the artificially created ego-based one; however, the latter is brittle, easily damaged (objects from outside can go away, like money; brand names can go out of fashion) *and so the ego is in a constant fight to maintain itself*. A heavily ego-based life is a stressful, and not a happy one. Just the sense of separation is enough to drive that unhappiness, but the ego goes much further than that, because of its need for constant enhancement and support. We all know people like this: they just can't stop dropping names, or buying things that make them look good, like cars, houses and so on. That their children are always "gifted," they are sure to let us know, and heaven help the educational psychologist who delivers the news that they are merely normal, or—gasp—"average"! The size and scope of their purchases and ego-based achievements depends on income, but the underlying process is the same. They use people like appendages rather than relating to them normally ("trophy wives" come to mind) and at work they are downright difficult to deal with, especially when in the role of boss, because *their pain is then spread around the team.* As we will see, social media has given ego-driven people even more and powerful new tools to play with. In most people, the ego is at least somewhat under control, but most of us can identify a time when we appeared to be in its grip. However, in some people it completely takes over control of its "host," and all hell breaks loose (which is why we have the phrase "egomaniac").

Ego and self-esteem are closely and *inversely related in some, but not all people.* Since ego is an "alternative me," those who do not feel so good about the original "me" (for whatever reason) gravitate toward this alternative as a good replacement for that original. This is why the ego is typically used—in these cases—to make the person "better than" others: because the original "me" *was seen to have failed and so was obviously defective, or "worse than."* In the conscious or unconscious conversations we all have with ourselves, the alternate "me" in those people becomes an identity that (they hope) can bring social success, acceptance and even love. It is not hard to imagine a person with significant psychological damage blaming themselves for this experience and vowing to remake "me" in what is hoped to be a more successful version. The ego helps them build this alternative identity, based on external identification and reinforcement.

Low self-esteem is not the only path to an ego-driven life, however, only one of the paths. Various researchers indicate that a culture based on "me," such as that which seems to have become established in the United States in the last 30 years, has produced not low self-esteem per se, but an inflated sense of "self" and entitlement among large sections of the population, along with an unwillingness to consider "others" in everyday life.[6] No doubt, therefore, ego has more than one path via which it can develop.

### How ego drives greed

> Earth provides enough to satisfy every man's need, but not every man's greed.
>
> Mahatma Gandhi[7]

Just as we will see when looking at the epidemic of narcissism soon, greed is one of many by-products of narcissism and its cousin, the ego. This is a simple mechanism that will become especially important in our discussion of how and why ego affects organizations. As we have seen, ego "takes over" its hosts, in more extreme cases, and drives them to fulfill its need to be "better than" others by constant acquisition of material goods and various status symbols, large and small. However this is a fool's errand: the status symbols of money and goods and designer jeans and thousands of Facebook friends work only for a while. *Ego is never satisfied!* Once something has been acquired, the ego tires of it quickly and drives its hosts in search of the next thing that will make them special, *which will ensure that they stay ahead of the pack.* Greed results; it is an inevitable outcome. Greed ensures that there will never be an end to the amount of money collected, and so on. Once one goal has been reached, a new one is set, as if the first one never mattered. Greed drives people to do things they might not otherwise have done, up to and including breaking the law. This is why we see people with so much, going out and doing crazy things to get even more.

Greed never ends well: in the investing world there is the phrase that *"bulls and bears make money, but pigs get slaughtered."* We have a similar farming example, which works well for both the investing and general organizational world:

Go in like a pig, come out like sausage.[8]

## Ego and the Crash

As James Gorman alludes to in his prescient piece quoted in Chapter 1, ego ("the individual as hero") was not just a bit part player in this financial drama, *it played a central role*. Gorman's comment shows us just how ego and the hero worship of the individual "star" had become embedded in the culture of financial firms, and his view is that this has to change. The idea that out-of-control ego has played a part in some societies for a while, and in the financial Crash in particular, is the focus of an interesting book titled *The Narcissism Epidemic: Living in the Age of Entitlement*.[9] The authors start with a stunning array of examples of such behavior, pulled from everyday American life:

On a reality TV show, a girl planning her Sweet Sixteen wants a major road blocked off so a marching band can precede her grand entrance on a red carpet. Five times as many Americans undergo plastic surgery and cosmetic procedures as ten years ago, and ordinary people hire fake paparazzi to follow them around to make them look famous. High school students physically attack classmates and post YouTube videos of the beatings to get attention. ... Although these seem like a random collection of current trends, all are rooted in a single underlying shift in American culture: the relentless rise of narcissism, a very positive and inflated view of self.[10]

Using data from a large proprietary survey of 37,000 college students, they back up their opinions with facts and demonstrate an upward trend of narcissism of significant proportions:

> [N]arcissistic personality traits rose just as fast as obesity from the 1980s till present, with the shift especially pronounced for women ... the rise in narcissism is accelerating.[11]

While Generation Y (born roughly between 1980 and 2000, hence the name "Millennials") is thought to be the most narcissistic, Baby Boomers and even earlier generations have also shown themselves to be quite selfish at times. For example, in recent polls in the US, the 65+ age group were adamantly against "government health care" for everyone, even though they themselves benefit enormously from it via the Medicare program!

Of particular importance for our discussion about the Crash of 2008, the authors leave no doubt as to the role of narcissism:

> At base, much of the economic meltdown of 2008 was caused by overconfidence and greed, two key symptoms of narcissism ... [N]arcissistic thinking works well in a rising market as bets pay off ... but ... is inherently an unstable, short term strategy.[12]

In some peoples' minds there is a fine line between ego and self-confidence, but they should not be confused with each other. Many professions require self-confidence to a high degree, and working in financial services is one of them; decisions are made using millions of pounds or euros of a firm's money, and those decisions have to be made quickly. This is not a profession for the faint of heart. But the ego is different altogether; it is something that can so emphasize "me" that "we" almost disappears, *whether "we" is the customer, the team of which that worker is part, the rest of the company or society as a whole.* The frequently used term that apparently was used by Wall Streeters a lot during the 1980s, "Masters of the Universe," demonstrates that some of these people think they are far better than the rest of us and do not have to play by our rules, a classic sign of inflated egos. Because of this, people can become victims of their own hubris and take off like lone rangers in directions that can have severe consequences for the rest of us. This is not limited to the US or Wall Street specifically, as the following spectacular examples demonstrate:

- "Despite surviving the Great Depression and both World Wars, [London-based bank] Barings was brought down in 1995 due to unauthorized trading by its head derivatives trader in Singapore, Nick Leeson ... Leeson's activities had generated losses totalling £827 million (US$1.3 billion), twice the bank's available trading capital. The collapse cost another £100 million. The Bank of England attempted a weekend bailout, but it was unsuccessful ... Barings was declared insolvent on 26 February 1995."[13]

- On October 5, 2010, "a French judge ... sentenced Jérôme Kerviel, the former Société Générale trader, to three years in prison and ordered him to repay €4.9 billion in restitution to the bank ... Mr. Kerviel, 33, whose €50 billion, or $69 billion at current exchange rates, in rogue dealings almost brought about the French bank's demise, was convicted on all counts of breach of trust, forgery and unauthorized use of computer systems."[14]

## Ego at work in the organization

### Ego and top management: Executive compensation

Ego and narcissism effects are not limited to catastrophic events that almost bring down, or actually do bring down, age-old banks. The ego is at work elsewhere, as the quote from James Gorman has suggested. One area inside the organization where the ego can be strongly in control, *in some countries*, is executive compensation. We will cover this topic at length here for three good reasons, which relate to the core thesis of the book:

- Excesses at the top of some organizations set the tone for the organization's culture at large and deliver a powerful, and negative, message.
- As a result, we believe *excesses in this area erode employee morale and engagement.*
- As a consequence of this, large-scale use of such excesses and their resulting side effects are hardly good for a nation's—or an individual organization's— competitiveness in world markets.

As we shall see, in the United States there is very little relationship between CEO pay and performance, even though those same CEOs often strongly support pay for performance for others further down the organization! In the financial services industry, *CEO compensation drives a culture that breeds entitlement further down the food chain.* Is it surprising, therefore, that James Gorman states that people who are not such stand-outs in his firm are receiving 10x the pay of those in relatively similar jobs outside of Wall Street? They expect it, they think they have earned it, even if the firm almost went under, and after all their CEO is "getting his"! Amazingly, many Wall Street bonuses remained *relatively* high all through the Recession, and quickly bounced back to record levels[15] as soon as the government rescue funds were paid back:

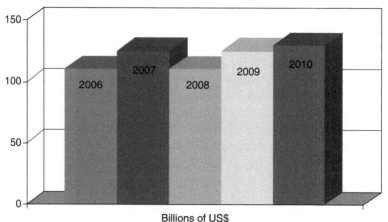

Billions of US$
Data: *Wall Street Journal*, February 2, 2011

*Chart 3.1*    Total compensation and benefits at 25 Wall Street firms

As we see from the chart, *even in the depths of the Crash, total Wall Street compensation dipped only to 2006 levels.* Let us recall that 2008 was a time of unprecedented bailouts and imminent failure (within one week, according to Fed Chairman Ben Bernanke) of 12 of the 13 top banks! 2008 was also a year when Wall Street profits, previously averaging over $50 billion a year, *actually went into a loss.* (To underline the disconnect between pay and performance demonstrated by these two years, 2006 showed profits of $80 billion.) In 2009 and 2010, with borrowed funds being paid back, pay and benefit numbers moved right ahead *to levels higher than before the Crash.*

By 2010, then, Wall Street pay was still in the stratosphere, with relatively little correlation to the effects of the Crash on the general population of workers. *But very recent data indicates that this party is coming to a close.* As a result of the delayed reaction to changes in regulation, de-leveraging in particular, the returns of the average financial services firm on Wall Street are tumbling; with worker pay based on a percentage of those returns, the effects will be quite dramatic. According to the Options Group, reported in the *The Wall Street Journal* and elsewhere,[16] 2011 bonuses on Wall Street could drop by up to 40%, and total pay 27–30%. Financial news channel CNBC even reported that this will affect the New York property market. "Damping" is bringing order to the chaos, but at what price? Only time will tell.

*How ego connects to executive pay*

Let's look at the mechanism whereby ego can drive executive pay.

The ego-driven individual loves the idea that "I" can make more than the next guy (or gal), and is horrified at the idea that "I" would ever make less!

Of course, the ego is canny, and needs to make sure that such excesses are guaranteed. Heaven forbid that the ego would not receive what it is worth! This means setting up their compensation in such a way that they are never affected by something as mundane as *performance*. That is far too risky and the ego cannot afford such risk and possible loss of status. Where do you think the "golden parachute" came from? Let's be clear about something: parachutes that are used for rescue purposes deploy when there has been a catastrophic failure. Whoever came up with the phrase knew what he or she was talking about, because the golden versions often do deploy when there has been, if not a catastrophe, at least a major failure. This is not pie in the sky: many, many times, at least in the US and UK, CEOs have parachuted out of companies in which they have drained shareholder value during their tenure, leaving behind shareholders and employees (often also shareholders themselves) who have no such escape mechanism. They left them behind in the plane! The ego has no problem with this because its sense of the "other" is limited. "Collateral damage" is invisible to the ego. Our case studies next show exactly what can happen.

*Executive compensation case studies*

First a disclaimer: the following is about a subset of CEOs. Not all CEOs are like this, and we do not in any way make that assumption. As organizational psychologists steeped in social science research we understand full well that samples should not be generalized to the whole unless they are truly representative. Many CEOs (and we have worked with a lot) are downright great people, generous, caring and absolutely dedicated to the welfare of their workforce. They don't have an ounce of greed in their bodies and they make sure they play by the same rules as those who work for them. Perhaps you work for one of these people, or are one of them yourself: this is not about them or you. This is a about a subset, enough of a group to make a difference in overall averages *in some countries*, and this subset has a mentality that damages the culture of their organizations, and along with that, worker engagement.

*Pay for performance, yes! But not for me ...*

The best-known executive compensation consultant in the US for many years, a man named Graef Crystal, or "Bud" to his friends and associates, is an interesting character, now retired. Crystal was responsible for many of the sophisticated pay and benefit plans that enriched CEOs and other members of top management at some of the best-known and most prestigious national and multinational companies in America. He was always on radio and TV as a guru on the subject of executive pay, usually having to justify what his clients were making. Then one day he had something that sounded almost like a spiritual revelation, which boiled down to one simple question: *what have I done?*

Crystal realized that he had been part of a huge arms race during which CEO pay had catapulted itself into the stratosphere, in relation to the pay of average workers. A simple chart brings this into perspective:[17-19]

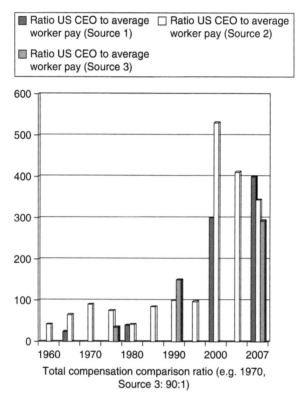

Chart 3.2    US CEO to average worker compensation ratio, 1960 to 2007
*Source*: Data Sources are shown in notes 17, 18 and 19.

The US *Fortune* magazine[20] provides an update for us for 2010, conveniently released right before publication of this book, in which the US CEO to worker ratio is an extraordinary *475:1*. Other countries that *Fortune* ranks against this number, and that show how far out of the norm it is, include:

Hong Kong: 44:1
Britain: 22:1
Canada: 20:1
France: 15:1
Germany: 12:1
Japan: 11:1

In 1960, the US ratio was 42:1 according to one source, and it moved up and down until a similar low in 1980. Then followed the period in which Graef Crystal certainly participated, where it peaked in the "dot-com" boom of 2000 and was still high just before the Crash, when ratios of around 400:1 or even greater were seen. *Incredibly, post-Crash (2010), according to the Fortune data, the US is at one of the highest ratios ever recorded.* If we take the average of the two data sources we have for 2000–2005, *the rise in this CEO to average worker pay ratio from 1980 to then is an astounding number: more than 900%!* This mirrors the gap between rich and poor, which is the subject of endless debate in the US, as it grows ever wider. The data on which we base this discussion is controversial as it covers the aggregate of many elements of executive pay, and not everyone agrees on what that should include. We have provided four sources of data to show that while there is no agreement on exact levels of CEO pay versus the average worker, *there is indeed a consensus on the huge rise in this ratio from 1990 until the present day.* Graef Crystal provides a very comprehensive model for what is included in CEO pay in his analysis (Source 3 in the chart), as follows:

- Base salary.
- Bonus for annual performance.
- The value at grant of free shares granted during the year.
- The estimated present value at grant (using the Black-Scholes model) of stock options granted during the year.
- The "target" value of prospectively-granted performance shares or units granted during the year.
- The present value of pension accruals for the particular year.
- And, as defined by the U.S. Securities and Exchange Commission, miscellaneous compensation.[21]

Now, as believers in fairness but *not equality of outcome*, we looked at all this with an open mind. Was it possible that executives were performing so much better than ever before, *even in relation to the increasing productivity of their own workforce*? Was this not just a case of "pay for performance," with the CEOs rightly getting rewarded for excelling? In one of his earlier moves after his revelation and movement to the "other side" of executive compensation, Crystal looked at exactly this issue. Here is what he found, as blogged by a newspaper reporter who used Crystal regularly as a source of business news, Phil Ebersole:

> What he concluded from his research is that there was no relation—not even a negative relation—between what CEOs and other corporate executives got, and the performance of their companies ... It was all random, he said.[22]

It seems incredible: *no relationship between pay and performance!* Yet were these not the very companies in which pay for performance had been implemented for almost everyone? Certainly everyone who was not on a union contract, which meant millions and millions of white-collar people and a similar amount of non-union blue-collar workers. Were these pay for performance programs not implemented with the full knowledge and approval of the same CEO? Exactly, and that was the ultimate irony of his finding: *"do what I say, and not what I do."* Chief among the culprits in this scenario was the "guaranteed bonus," which formed part of the initial contract. This meant, rain or shine, profit or loss, triumph or disaster, *it had to be paid!* Failure to pay this meant a guaranteed lawsuit.

What does drive executive pay, though, if not performance? What drives it is something the ego would love: size! When a rank order correlation is created from Graef Crystal's data, between size rank and ratio of CEO to worker pay, the correlation is more than a negative 0.9. In other words, the bigger the size (lower rank no.) of the company, the greater the ratio between CEO and worker pay. This gives an even stronger connection to his data than the analysis he himself did: he reported that when looked at on a much deeper level than ranking, size accounted for some 30% of the ratio. As an example, Crystal found that the largest US companies in 2007 had CEO pay to average worker ratios of no less than 525, *a record level since he had started to look at the data early in his career.*[23] Performance, as we have pointed out, is completely below the radar.

Let's be clear here that we are not talking about the late Steve Jobs and about Sergey Brin, the geniuses who founded the now-iconic companies they used to, or still lead, and who deserve every bit of positive press (and dollar) they have received; we are not talking about the hundreds of thousands of less well-known entrepreneurs who risk everything for their dream. We're talking about a different animal here: *the hired hands brought in as CEOs.* They came in with a big blaze of publicity and then often had mixed results. As examples of this we can look at Bob Nardelli at Home Depot, Carly Fiorina at Hewlett-Packard and quite a few others. Their Boards were acquiescent to the point of giving them a contract that no average worker could receive: a fail-safe golden parachute, which translated into "you win, you win; you fail, you win." That is exactly what happened in our two examples; under Nardelli, Home Depot stock went DOWN by 8% in an up market but he made $240 in total compensation from December 2000 until his exit in January 2007. His exit package was an *additional $210 million.*[24] That's right, two hundred and ten million dollars. Under Fiorina, HP stock also went down.

When Fiorina became CEO in July, 1999, HP's stock price was $52 per share, and when she left over five years later in February, 2005, it was $21 per share—a loss of over 60% of the stock's value. During this same time period, HP competitor Dell's stock price increased from $37 to $40 per share.

For this remarkable performance, a *60% drop in share price*, her exit package was $42 million.[25] At GM, Rick Wagoner's planned $20 million pension was interrupted and probably doomed by the company's bankruptcy;[26] his contribution to GM's performance resulted in a *drop of 96% in the stock price under his tenure*. Now let's imagine a GM worker in the paint shop with a 96% defect rate; would he have had the continued employment enjoyed by Wagoner, along with a nice pension waiting for him? We don't think so.

Even Jack Welch, once untouchable as the glorified CEO of the American giant, GE (and with some justification, based on performance[27]), severely damaged his image with his $8 million/year retirement package,[28] which even included *flowers and wine* in one of his six luxury residences plus offices, all paid for by future GE shareholders.[29] This was only brought to light by his divorce, and created such an uproar that even the SEC (government financial regulator) got involved with GE, giving it a slap on the corporate wrist for lack of disclosure.[30] Welch and the company were shamed into giving a big part of it back. As we travel around and meet various people on planes, trains and in professional meetings who have knowledge of this type of situation, the Welch divorce is often mentioned as a watershed in the *"executive excess"* stakes. Interestingly, these types of negative comments come equally from politically left and right leaning types; *it is an issue that appeals across ideological lines*. A look at the three pages of charts that itemize the perks Welch and his soon-to-be-ex were to have received from GE shareholders is simply breathtaking, and well worth further study.[31] Need to take a little trip? The company 737 is at your disposal! Can't make it to the airport? No worries, the helicopter will come for you! Postage for your mail? That would be too much of a hardship—GE will pay for it!

Apparently, it wasn't enough that he left GE with at least $720 million[32] in stock.[33]

Of course, all sorts of justifications are put forward as to why CEOs might deserve these levels of pay, such as the increasing size of organizations, their complexity and so on. Rather than repeat them all here, we recommend reading a remarkable blog by a CEO who decided to go in another direction, John Mackey of Whole Foods Market (WF).[34] In it, Mackey demolishes the arguments made to justify these differences and talks convincingly about his policy at WF: no one may make more than 19 times the average worker's pay, as a matter of principle, to bolster internal equity *and what he calls "solidarity" with his workforce*. While this word might make some shudder, let us remind readers that Mackey is currently a darling of the *Wall Street Journal* readers, whom he has charmed with his common sense approach to health benefits at WF. Don't be fooled by the tree-hugging image of organic food and soy-everything: Mackey is a hard-nosed entrepreneur and capitalist who understands the huge benefits that accrue to those organizations that really do "put people first." He epitomizes the "American Dream," but with a soft spot for his workforce. This combination has made WF the biggest organic grocer in the world. Not a bad outcome for the skeptics of such an approach. For this reason, *and his proven long-term success*, we decided to feature Mackey and Whole Foods Market in Chapter 5 of this book.

Others have also tackled the arguments used to defend CEO pay with similar gusto as Mackey, arguing that this is not a case of supply and demand of talent and so on.[35] For example, the supply of talented MBAs is vaster than ever, with people coming from all over the world. Surely there are enough from which to find top management for the worlds' organizations? Why, too, would this be such an issue in one country (the US) if it were a worldwide problem finding such talent? Do the Germans not have talented people too, running BMW, Siemens and Daimler AG These are also very large companies, yet their top management pay is modest even under those circumstances.

Although seen as a clone of the US by many, an outpost of "cowboy capitalism" in Europe, at that time the UK was far behind it in executive pay. Its ratio may have climbed somewhat since 2004 but the Crash and its after-effects seem to be having an influence there, although in ways that seem government mandated, which is against our principles. For example, ideas are being floated as we write, that no government official may make more than 20 times that of his or her co-workers' average pay in the public sector. Whether these will be implemented remains to be seen.[36] Meanwhile don't expect any US-style CEO to worker pay ratios elsewhere in Europe: if a French CEO were to demand 300 times the average worker's pay, you would see demonstrations on the streets of Paris. Germans would be outraged, and given austerity measures in Spain, Greece, Ireland and Portugal, such pay levels there would be unthinkable.

Now we see the US public mood swinging heavily against such excesses: no longer able to tap rising house values, and more scared of facing unemployment, if not already there, the view from Main Street toward the corporate world's compensation game is decidedly sour. Who can blame people, when their taxes are being used to bail out some of those who are the main perpetrators? Perhaps Americans will indeed look back one day at this period that resulted in the Crash and say, *"yes that was the time when we changed this whole fad of glorifying some of our CEOs and brought them back down to reality."* Reality is that too many CEOs underperformed but were paid as if they were superstars. Recent data does show some shift in the financial services industry, as a result of extreme government pressure plus public opinion: some 60% of senior executives in that sector are now deferring bonuses, but much more remains to be done, such as adjusting the bonuses based on the risks taken to earn them.[37]

*So where does the ego fit into all this?* By default: when performance cannot be counted on to explain such generosity to US CEOs, we are left with the fact that they felt entitled, that they felt they deserved such treatment. Clearly, this sense of entitlement has mushroomed in the last 30 years, as our data show. But this goes beyond entitlement: remember the definition of narcissism, which includes greed? Can we really say that this situation is not at least influenced by greed? We do not believe we can. Of course, executive compensation consultants are often to blame too: they give too much away because they are often paid by the very people whose pay they are setting, and the pressure to give in is clearly unbearable. Who will bite the hand that feeds her? We know from our own experience in this area that there has been pressure to deliver a pay plan that is *nearly always going to pay off.* Can this pressure be removed from these consultants? Better that they be employed at "arm's length" by the Board. But wait a minute. Isn't the Board often selected by the CEO as well? Does it not serve at his (usually a male) pleasure? No wonder people think this game is fixed!

The idea that executive pay is a big issue for organizations is not at all new and has been commented on by some leading gurus and business leaders. As we have seen, the issue of pay fairness even crosses typical political party lines and moves into the ranks of people we might not expect to have these views. The eminent management professor Peter Drucker said that a 20:1 ratio of CEO to worker pay was appropriate, and that number is often quoted and used by others.[38] Drucker was very worried about the effects of a widening pay gap on society, and held onto this view for a long time; long enough to see some of his quite dire predictions come true, as we see here:

> I have serious reservations about capitalism as a system because it idolizes economics as the be all and end all of life. It is one-dimensional. For example, I have often advised managers that a 20-1 salary ratio is the limit beyond which they cannot go if they don't want resentment and falling morale to hit their companies. I worried back in the 1930s that the great inequality generated by the industrial revolution would result in so much despair that something like fascism would take hold. Unfortunately, I was right.[39]

The US Banker J. P. Morgan decreed that no one in his companies could earn more than 20 times the pay of the lowest paid worker. Even former Federal Reserve Chairman and darling of the right Alan Greenspan said something quite interesting on the subject of America's widening income gap: "it is not the type of thing which a democratic society ... can really accept without addressing."[40] Indeed the well-known Gini rating of pay equity[41] shows that America looks more like a dictatorship than a democracy, lining up nicely with Iran on that count.[42]

Is there any light at the end of this tunnel? There is! The US financial regulator, the SEC, is about to require full disclosure of the ratio of CEO pay to average worker, something that the *The New York Times* refers to as a "Name and

Shame" process.[43] Perhaps this light will cleanse the practices seen in the US and bring them more in line with levels others around the world seem to find quite sufficiently motivating!

### Ego, mergers and acquisitions

Is merger and acquisition (M&A) activity always done for the right reasons? Can we really suggest that the ego might be involved? Let's first look at whether mergers and acquisitions work. That's right, for some reason most big mergers and acquisitions do not generally add value to the organizations that conduct them.[44] Listen to Wharton accounting Professor Robert Holthausen, who teaches courses on Mergers and Acquisitions Strategy:

> Noting that there have been "hundreds of studies" conducted on the long-term results of mergers, Holthausen says that researchers estimate the range for failure is between 50% and 80%.[45]

Management professor Martin Sikora, editor of *Mergers & Acquisitions: The Dealmaker's Journal*, says that *"one-third of mergers create shareholder value, whereas one-third destroy value, and another third don't meet expectations."*[46]

There are many examples of spectacular failure, where expected synergies never materialized and the acquirer's stock price was depressed for many years; Sprint's 2005 acquisition of wireless innovator Nextel Communications in the US was a perfect example, of which one of us had personal experience as a customer. Prior to the Nextel acquisition by Sprint, Nextel was a scrappy company with an excellent product, superior customer service and unique features to which millions of customers seemed to be very committed. Although partly cobbled together with wireless spectrum bought from taxi companies, Nextel could deliver its "walkie-talkie" connection almost instantly across the thousands of miles of US mainland and even to the Hawaiian Islands and parts of Mexico and South America. The familiar Nextel "chirp" indicating a walkie-talkie connection could be heard everywhere. All that disappeared when Sprint bought the company and both it and its parent went on a slow and painful downward slide from which it may never recover.

Now we are not saying that Sprint's CEO at the time bought Nextel for egoistic reasons. We are saying that there must be a reason why the "50–80%" failure rate exemplified by Sprint and Nextel exists. Corporate culture clashes exist, for sure, and these are underestimated at one's peril, going into a merger or acquisition. National cultures can clash too when cross-border M&A is carried out. Plain old bad management plays its role, such as buying a company that is not really a strategic fit, even though some were convinced it was. But clearly it is possible for an extremely persuasive CEO to win over his or her Board (often selected by that CEO) into conducting an M&A activity, *and create nothing more than a larger organization.* While a failure in terms of stock price, customer satisfaction and many other external measures, this may not be a failure for that CEO. Recall the fact that Graef Crystal demonstrated the huge effect of size (not performance) on executive pay. A much larger company crafted as a result of M&A provides just the opportunity to rise up into the higher pay ratios we have seen, especially in the US. Is it possible to go into this form of corporate Russian Roulette with only a 33% chance of creating value and a greater chance of destroying it, just for the reason of size? The ego would say, yes that is a great reason to do this; it will enhance the prestige of said CEO and best of all, increase his pay! If it doesn't work, don't worry too much, there is that golden parachute waiting to deploy.

### Ego and mid-level management: The "boss from hell"

Imagine the worst boss you ever had, was she or he loaded down with ego? Here are some of the symptoms:

- She takes credit for projects that you started and carried out.
- He never hires people smarter than himself.
- He "licks up" and "kicks down" in the organization structure.
- She cannot take criticism.
- He is a perfectionist and one can never "do it well enough" for him.
- She never allows anyone else to make any significant decision in her area.

Welcome to the *ego-driven boss from hell*! The ego possession makes him or her feel extremely vulnerable because identification with all the "things" in life is like building a house on sand. Underneath this vulnerability and fear (*which we often never see, only the symptoms of ego-affliction are visible*) this boss lives on the knife-edge, always having to make sure than *nothing, nothing at all*, upsets this fragile status quo. At work this means always having to check up on you to make sure you will not show this boss up in a bad light.

You can hopefully see the short step to engagement: you are there at work to share your talents and skills and help the organization succeed. You love your job, but your boss, *oh dear, your boss is an egomaniac!* You didn't know that at first, your radar didn't send out a code red alert when you had the interview, but you found out later that something was very, very wrong. All the things that we described earlier started to happen. You arrived at the job ready, willing and able to engage but now—now the thing you most want to engage in is finding a new boss there or perhaps leaving the organization for a new job.

As we saw with the list of management traits previously, excessive control is one sign that the ego is lurking inside a manager. Ask an ego-driven manager to give up some control, to delegate, to flatten the structure and let some teams manage themselves, for example, and you will be met with a show of horror and logical justification as to why that should *never* happen. But these aren't the real reasons: under the surface, the ego abhors loss of control because of its fragile nature and high levels of fear, and the sense that *such delegation might lead to loss of status in some way.*

One of the problems in the world of work is that ego-driven top management often picks those like themselves for other management jobs; they call it a "nice fit." We call it, *extending the ego-model out into the whole organization.* This means that in these environments you are unlikely to get far by complaining about such a person, even if you describe what they do: top management will laugh and say that that's quite normal, healthy behavior. From where some of them stand, it is.

**Ego and the individual at work: The "co-worker from hell"**

Ego is by no means limited to management in the workplace. It is just that in management it has power, and scope. This gives it the chance to do some serious damage. There are also, of course, ego-driven co-workers, who may not have much power over others but are a pain to work with, and manage. They drain the energy of the group and occupy too much time of the manager. As host of an occupying force, their energy is not going to be focused on your organization and its goals, nearly as much as someone who does not have this trait. Instead the ego-driven employee will spend inordinate amounts of time on other things, to satisfy the insatiable needs of this force that has them in its grip. We humans think we know ourselves as we get older, but often we do not; instead, we continue to do things that the ego demands in order for it to continue to exist. Let's look at some of these behaviors that might show up in your current or prospective employees or, yes, even you:

- Sheila has a compulsive drive to up her personal Twitter and Facebook connections, even asking people she knows almost nothing about to become "friends" and competing with others who seem to have "made it" on these platforms. As a result social networking takes up a significant part of her workday, even though much of it may not be business related. (How's that for a productive day? You added 20 "friends" but got nothing done at work!) Like many good activities and things in life, Facebook or Twitter can also become an addiction, and although Sheila does not think she is addicted to anything, she nonetheless feels a compulsion to act out this behavior. Unconsciously, Sheila has a deep belief that if she has 5000 Facebook friends she will have a certain worth or value that was lacking when the count was five. When she reaches that number, however, after a painfully short celebration, she finds that it does not "work" and she is no happier; unfortunately she is not allowed more than 5000 friends by Facebook,[47] so is "stuck" there. Unless she has the courage, support and emotional intelligence to look within, Sheila will soon start to look for another temporary and fragile external solution to her inner problem.

- Fred treats his bosses like parents, even gravitating to a boss whose style most (unconsciously) reminds him of a parent with whom he had problems. This same mechanism is at work with the woman who marries a man who treats her like her father did, of course. It's familiar, it's what she is used to, what she thinks she deserves (good or bad, we are not saying this is always a bad thing, it's just a common thing). In the organization, we see this all the time. We also see a more extreme version, where a mild-mannered boss can be seen as a tyrant by an ego-possessed worker, whose bad childhood experience of "authority" makes anyone in an authority position "bad" like the parent. This is of course a failure of perception, a projection of the parent onto someone who may not deserve it at all. Of course, in Fred's case, since he always seems to gravitate to people who are actually like his Dad, the perception could be close to reality! Fred sees himself as a victim of these types of people, but of course he is not: he continually chooses them. Until he understands his choices and why he makes them, he will continue to do this, and his organization will get less of his talent and energy and more of his childhood struggles.

- Mike expects to be rewarded for just showing up. His ego has given him its inflated sense of "worth" and entitlement, which has overwhelmed its host. This is not to be confused with self-confidence or real self-esteem. The ego version is unrealistic and unearned; but if this is pointed out, the ego will react harshly, to say the least! Unfortunately, Mike does not have a solid sense of himself as a good or capable person, so external signs are constantly solicited and he pressures his manager in ways that she finds very irritating. In Mike's case his problem was exacerbated by growing up at a time when his peer group of "Trophy Kids" was given awards for placing fourth in a race, for example. Constant positive feedback, which his ego demanded, was actually provided by a (temporary) cultural phenomenon, the expectations of which organizations still struggle with today.

- Johnny makes a confrontation of everything and plays to win at all times, even when this is not at all appropriate. This drives other team members crazy; why can't he relax and have fun sometimes, or let someone else shine? Because his ego will not allow it. His ego requires constant proof that he, Johnny, is the best! Johnny's ego scoffs at the idea of making room for, or celebrating, the success of others, seeing such apparent generosity as "weakness."

- Christine cannot receive anything but an "exceeds expectations" rating on the dreaded annual performance review. Unlike the normal disappointment that might come to those who are rated "average" (although never using that word, always euphemistically called "meets expectations"), Christine goes into a major funk each time and gets into a verbal fight with her manager. She also gets seriously discouraged, instead of being able to bounce back and excel based on what she has learned. This in turn reduces her chances of genuinely deserving a hike in the rating next time.

In each and every case here, the ego has taken over an individual. In one way or another, and there are several ways in which this happens, a false and very fragile self has been created and maintained, sometimes for decades, and ends up causing havoc everywhere this person lives, including at work. The amount of time and energy that goes into managing the hosts and the egos themselves is uncountable, because it is so widespread. Listen to this:

> In a 2011 survey in the US conducted by a temporary work agency, *Accountemps* and reported online, "managers were asked, 'What percentage of management time is wasted resolving staff personality conflicts?' The mean response was 18 percent."[48]

Almost 20% of management time dealing with workers' personality conflicts? It is an awful number. Imagine what could be achieved in that time, which would not lessen but *improve* the morale and engagement of those teams.

As we have seen, the constant focus on "self" demanded by the ego leaves little room for "other," which is very damaging in an organization, but not only internally: *the customer satisfaction consequences of such ego-driven (and often disgruntled) employees are off the charts.*[49] Whether the employees got to this disgruntled state under the pressure of their own ego or in exasperation at having to work for an ego-driven manager, the reason that the customer experience is eroded is the effect of all of this negative experience on the *employees' engagement levels.*

### Ego and worker engagement: Making the connection

> Organization: "A structure through which individuals *cooperate systematically* to conduct business."[50]

> (emphasis added)

It is not a big logical step to go from ego existing inside the organization to its effects on engagement. *Ego and engagement are polar opposites: engagement is about "we" and ego is about "me."* If we look at the aforesaid dictionary definition of the word *organization* we see quite clearly that organizations are also about "we," or at least they ought to be, bringing co-workers together to achieve their mission, "engaging" with customers, suppliers and stockholders, etc. This means that engagement fits naturally into the organizational environment as a "we"-oriented process, making everything run better. No wonder performance is so enhanced. That is, until engagement hits the ego. Note that *organization* is specifically defined in terms of *cooperation*; and as the insightful spiritual writer and teacher Eckhart Tolle has pointed out in his valuable book *A New Earth: Awakening to Your Life's Purpose*, cooperation and the ego are like oil and water:

> Cooperation is alien to the ego, except when there is a secondary motive. The ego doesn't know that the more you include others, the more smoothly things flow and the more easily things come to you. When you give little or no help to others or put obstacles in their path, the universe—in the form of people and circumstances—is little or no help to you because you have cut yourself off from the whole. The ego's unconscious core feeling of "not enough" causes it to react to someone else's success as if that success had taken something away from "me."[51]

As we have seen, ego operates on multiple levels of an organization:

- At the top, it can drive the culture, the *"way we do things around here."* Among those things that are "done" is the way people at the top are paid, including how much and how related that is to performance. The culture is affected more than that though: is it all about internal competition ("dog eat dog") and individual "heroes"? That is a sure sign of ego woven into that culture, a reflection of someone's "values." That culture can and often does become self-perpetuating, as when people are hired or promoted by an ego-driven leader in his or her own image.
- Some organizations that have had a long history of building successful, people-oriented cultures can make the huge mistake of hiring someone at the top who may be a tough, get-it-done manager, but whose ego-based behavior (including pay demands) shatters the values of those organizations. This leaves behind a trail of cynicism among the workforce and can destroy the culture that took years to nurture and grow.
- At the middle of the organization, ego can drive mid-level managers who protect their "empires" or "silos," and keep a lid on their staff's ability to shine too brightly, lest that shine should make the manager look dull in comparison. The ego would not like that at all.
- At the individual worker level, we have some people whose ego takes up the majority of a manager's time, which could be spent so much better on sharing successes and working with the team in a more expansive and engaging way, rather than just putting out one person's fires.

How do we know that all this affects worker engagement? Because we have measured it in the data from countless surveys; we have read it in the comments of people writing in the open-ended section of those surveys; we have heard it in hundreds upon hundreds of focus groups; and we have heard it from so many people whom we meet on planes and trains and in organizations around the word. As soon as they hear that we work in organizational morale and engagement, they almost beg us to come to their workplace to help! The stories they tell us often speak of out-of-control egos in the workplace.

We do not, however, have to rely on either our own data or on purely anecdotal evidence that some of these situations are disengaging for workers. Let's take the issue of executive pay, for example:

> Studies confirm that business performance deteriorates when pay differentials become excessive. In a study of over 100 businesses (producing everything from kitchen appliances to truck axles), researchers found that the greater the wage gap between managers and workers, the lower their product's quality. Businesses with the greatest inequality were plagued with a high employee turnover rate.[52]

Study author David Levine was quoted as saying something very interesting: "These organizations [the ones with a high manager to worker pay ratio] weren't able to sustain a workplace of people with shared goals."[53] In other words, they were not able to tell everyone "we're all in this together" with a straight face.

In an interesting and well-controlled German study from 2009, researchers looked at the perception by workers of CEO pay as being "fair" and related it to absenteeism, which they point out is well documented in Germany as a good measure of morale and engagement. While controlling for other factors that might influence absenteeism, such as health, job security and even political views, the authors make a statement that is quite striking compared to a typical, carefully worded academic study:

> [T]hese results imply massive behavioral consequences of perceiving the income of top managers to be unfairly high.[54]

The fact that they found clear evidence that people there are much more likely to be absent from work when they perceive management's pay to be "unfair" is very interesting. It would support what some long-established theories have put forward[55] that absenteeism and similar behaviors are an effort by the workers to "level the playing field," to make up for what is *perceived to be an imbalance.*

The conclusion of this study, completed at the height of the Crash, was interesting and directly relates to our own observations: that not only do people object when such financial crises occur (in Germany, with street demonstrations), but that in normal times "perceived unfairness of CEO pay may also lead to 'hidden' protest behavior that bears the potential of large economic costs, *even outside times of financial crisis*"[56] (emphasis added).

## Conclusions: Ego at work in the organization

About this time you might be getting the impression that ego is endemic in many organizations and has some very negative effects. Indeed, we would go further than that and say:

1. *Excessive ego is one of the most damaging factors for any organization's culture and its level of morale and engagement; in turn this cannot have anything but a negative effect on the organization's performance.*

Ego unleashed on an organization by a janitor in a factory is one thing; by a CEO it is quite another. As we look at organizational effects of seriously ego-based behavior, therefore, we need to consider scale. The janitor may be a pain for his co-workers and boss, but he cannot change his organization's culture just because he is an egomaniac. The CEO, on the other hand, *can change the whole culture and thousands of workers' lives as a result.* As we saw from the Crash, depending on the industry and the size and scope of the organizations involved, this can have much broader side effects:

2. *Ego-based work cultures, in large enough organizations, can cause serious damage to the broader society.*

Ego has to do with "me," and "we" is secondary or sometimes almost nonexistent. This is its fatal and most dangerous flaw, and one that must be mitigated if we are to build a sustainable and engaging work culture for the competitive future that lies ahead.

# Part II
# What Can We Do To Change?

# 4
# Balancing **Me** and **We**: Building a Sustainable, High Engagement Work Culture

In December of 1995 a factory called Malden Mills in the US state of Massachusetts burned to the ground in the largest fire that had happened in that state for 100 years. Malden Mills was famous for its *Polartec®* fabric, used by military and civilian clothing manufacturers to insulate garments against cold weather. Its owner and CEO, Aaron Feuerstein, was the third generation of his family to run the operation, the largest employer by far in an economically depressed area. For some time before that, this type of textile business, which Malden Mills represented, had been moving to lower cost centers in Asia, and the fire certainly represented a chance for Mr. Feuerstein to collect his insurance money and do the same, or simply retire. *He did neither.*

Mindful of the 1500 people whose livelihoods depended on this factory, he set out to rebuild on the same spot; but even more than that *he paid all his workers for two months even though they had nothing to do.* This was the year-end holiday period, after all. This cost Mr. Feuerstein some $25 million, a sum that he seemed to be glad to invest. Lauded by the press and then-President Clinton, Mr. Feuerstein was quoted as saying:

> "I got a lot of publicity. And I don't think that speaks well for our times," says Feuerstein. "At the time in America of the greatest prosperity, the god of money has taken over to an extreme."[1]

Mr. Feuerstein's actions saved the jobs of his workers for many years but the story does not ultimately have a Hollywood ending. The garment industry had been leaving the United States for years even before the fire, due to extreme cost differences between US and overseas factories, and in the end, financial pressures made it close and its assets were sold.[2] But the values reflected in *this man's action are an inspiration* and a counterbalance to the recent events of the Crash. They show us that such values are out there among owners

81

of businesses, among CEOs; surely there are many Aaron Feuersteins in the organizational world, perhaps not having to endure devastating fires like he did, but nonetheless totally dedicated to the well-being of their workers and with little or no ego and greed to be seen in their actions. So in spite of our trip through the dark world of ego and its trails of damage to societies and their organizations, we remain optimistic that all is not lost. Indeed, while mindful of the negative consequences of the Crash on millions of people around the world, we are grateful that things have been exposed, which may help move us forward. As they say at your local gym: *No Pain, No Gain.*

To take advantage of this opportunity, of this time of seemingly endless and quite dramatic natural and man-made events presenting themselves just about everywhere, we believe we can learn from the Feuersteins and others, build on the generous examples they have set, and *find a better way of doing things* in our organizational world. With change in the air, *we see the possibility of a different culture in our workplaces*, one that is sustainable, protects us at least somewhat from the downside of what we have discussed so far, and *results in high worker engagement and high performance.*

## The sustainable, high engagement work culture: Requirements

We have previously (in Chapter 2) had an extensive discussion of culture at work and worker engagement, defining them and examining their origins. We looked at worldwide trends in engagement in order to make the argument that *in many places* all is not well in this facet of work life, and why that might be so. Here we begin the prescriptive part of our book, where we set out the conditions and steps necessary for organizations to create *cultures that work for everyone*. This requires that we leverage our pyramid model of how a workplace culture becomes one in which people wish to engage. We will set out some basic requirements for this culture:

- It must be do-able, not "pie-in-the-sky":
  We do not wish to propose a starry-eyed dream of organizational perfection, which has never been tested in the real world. Instead we much prefer something that actually works and is being used now.
- It must create winners of all stakeholders:
  Workers, managers, leaders, customers, suppliers, shareholders and the larger community—the culture must support the idea that all must be able to "win."
- It must be convincingly worthwhile to our organizational leaders:
  No organization will embark on any effort to remake its culture if there is no return in store for this effort. This is not a touchy-feely exercise; it is *mission critical*. It has *significant return on investment, in terms of performance.*

Organizations must be convinced of these facts or they will never try to change.

- It must NOT depend on further government regulation:
Regulation is already in place around the world's industrial economies—far better to actually use the regulations that are already there, rather than allow them to be circumvented. No UK Premier League football match would ever be allowed to get around the rules of football for a particular game; so why should we allow this with our organizations? Government regulation should stop at the point where it makes the "game" *fair, as we have defined that word* (*not* equal); beyond that, its effects become a burden on the animal spirits in the organizational world that have given us so much and that we need, to move us forward.

- It must follow universal principles:
The universe, "nature," call it what you will, seems to have figured things out quite well. Easy for we humans to say, as one of its grateful creations! In spite of its apparent chaos, to some human minds anyway, it actually operates on an exquisite level of *balance* and uses various means to ensure that that balance stays in place. It also takes giant leaps into what looks to us like the "unknown," but which are in fact still guided by its own rules. We would be—and have been—foolish to ignore this fact in our organizational life.[3] Letting ourselves be guided by these principles would help us avoid some of the mistakes we have made and which recently almost sank our financial institutions.

- It must be proven to support worker well-being, including health and happiness:
We believe that following a path guided by universal principles and best management practices is *a recipe for well-being, including happiness.* Happiness at work? Some people will say that is an oxymoron! Yet it is a hot topic and rightly so, as we shall see later and have discussed at length elsewhere.[4,5] Surely a work culture that does not leave its workers with a greater sense of well-being, *with all the benefits that accrue from that,* is not worth having. Who in their "right mind" can spend eight hours a day or more in an environment where they are unhappy and become *"dis-eased"*? And from where they take the effects of this home to create yet more damage? Who can create such an environment? Yet far too many do one or even both of these things.

- It must emphasize *emotional intelligence* as much or more than IQ:
If we are to build a culture that supports high engagement, we cannot rely simply on normal intelligence to get us there. Research shows that *emotional intelligence (EQ)*[6] is far more important for many aspects of organizational life, especially for managers. Knowing this, and designing our organizations around this, is truly a "smart" thing to do.

- It must ensure that organizational life plays out *fairly*, with outcomes produced only by performance factors such as effort, intelligence (IQ/EQ), commitment, courage/risk taking, and nothing else:
  Knowing the "right people" at your office or factory to help you get salary increases and promotions must score you no points under this culture; neither must going out for a drink and eating pizza every Friday night with your boss. Every effort must be made to put performance front and center, with high levels of transparency so that all can see that this is so.
- It must adapt and strengthen capitalism, not try and replace it:
  We have no intention of proposing anything that would kill the golden goose that has spawned and supported prosperity around the world, namely capitalism. Instead we wish to see capitalism reoriented and revitalized with the full power that people like Adam Smith intended for it. Why try to take us back to failed approaches such as state control of all means of production and commerce or worse? We have seen the results of that and they did not produce what people or society needed. Capitalism is not perfect, as everyone knows and we have detailed here. *But, like any human creation, it can be fixed.*
- It must work for everyone, not just some; "we" and not just "me." Egos should be checked at the door:
  Engagement does not happen across a large percentage of the workforce if the internal culture is "me" focused. The cultural approach we propose has no room for "hero" stock traders who destroy institutions and bring the rest of us to the brink of disaster; no room for self-centered leaders who live under different rules than those they impose on the rest of their workers. Clearly, we need more of the type of leader who thinks of "we" before she thinks of "me." The culture we embrace will reject the ego-based leaders or workers who grind down the team's sense of well-being with their behavior.
- It must create the conditions for increased worker and customer engagement:
  Our organizational leaders need to know that in the case of any successful work culture, *the very reason for its success is that workers have chosen to become highly engaged.*[7] As a result of this, customer satisfaction and engagement increases, productivity and profitability are enhanced and worker health is significantly improved. A work culture that does not first produce the conditions for increased worker engagement is not worth having, because all of the positive and valuable by-products will not be realized.
- It must bring out the best in people, and capitalize on inherent talents that are so often neglected:
  To be successful, this work culture must view workers as valuable and precious, respect their humanity and their unique talents, and truly treat them as if they are the bedrock of the organization. This is not a stretch or a form

of pretense; it is reality. It is achieved not with words in annual reports or in training materials, *but with deeds carried out on a daily basis.*

- It must be measured, tracked over time and *enforced*:
Both culture and engagement can be easily measured by asking everyone in the organization various questions, in a formal and (usually, but not always) confidential survey format. This enables one to know crucial information about the place from where one is starting, how far one has traveled and whether one has reached certain goals and much more. *It is essential to any serious effort to change.* Some organizations believe that they cannot, or should not measure these kinds of things. This is a big mistake. *Enforcement* sounds like a somewhat ominous word but simply means that such is the importance of values, culture and engagement for the very best organizations that they do not tolerate violations in this area. *Neither should you.*

## The sustainable, high engagement work culture: Building on universal principles

In 1987, Michael Douglas, playing the character Gordon Gekko, uttered the famous words that came to symbolize Wall Street for so many people, about *greed being good.* The original quote is worth *googling*, because it is cleverly wrapped in a larger sentence in which greed is made out to almost be the natural order of things, the very reason for mankind's success in the lottery of life, the very basis of evolution!

The character of Gordon Gekko was rumored to be based on Ivan Boesky,[8] and Michael Milken, both convicted of financial crimes, with a little bit of well-known Wall Street financier Carl Icahn thrown in.[9] While Michael Douglas earned an Oscar for a powerful performance in this film, if there had been an award for factual correctness based on the previous quote, it would not have gone to this film. The quote has been endlessly repeated because it captured the *Zeitgeist* of Wall Street at that time so well. Are we surprised that the quote is as current now as it was then? Not really.

It is a clever statement because it purports to build on lofty universal principles to justify what is in fact criminal behavior (as depicted in the film). Trust the crafty and occasionally devious human mind to come up with that one. At first, it might even sound reasonable, in that, yes the universe is a pretty competitive place. But when we really look a little closer, is it *greed* that we are seeing? Or is the universe, judging by that tiny part of it we occupy, more of a delicate balancing act than one based on greed? Which animal, aside from humans, is greedy? Which one gathers far more than it needs? Do lions eat until they grow grotesquely fat? That would be counterproductive when it came to the next dash for a fast-moving meal. Do squirrels store enough nuts for the next 25 winters? Do eagles build nests that are far, far larger than anything they need to lay eggs and bring them to term, so that they impress other eagles?

When we look at our human selves in this context, we sometimes look a little ridiculous. Not because we have striven to bring some of ourselves up from subsistence living to a more comfortable existence, but just how far we have gone at the extremes. When we then turn around and justify what we have done by saying that those extremes conform to universal laws, we extend that to the realm to absurdity!

The fact is that it is much more than greed that has moved mankind into the pole position of the animal kingdom, as Gordon Gekko implies in the film. Instead, life is based on a *balance* of many factors, especially between *competition and cooperation*. To illustrate this we will draw on the work of someone who has given this a lot of thought for many years. He came up with the idea of *co-opetition*.

### Co-opetition: It is everywhere

The best ideas are always the most simple and the most widely applicable. They explain what we see in the world and bring order and sense to it. We believe that *co-opetition* is one of those ideas and is highly relevant to our discussion of organizational culture. We have a man named V. Frank Asaro to thank for this word, for his many hours of scholarly research and productive thinking and a recent book on the subject.[10] A lawyer by training and profession, but an endlessly curious intellectual and inventor by nature, Frank came up with this concept between 1980 and 1990 as he struggled to explain the universe to himself. We cannot guarantee that others may not have used this word somewhere in the world before then, but from a cursory search he looks like the first, but certainly not the last.[11] He processed what he saw with the complex matrix of social, political, anthropological, philosophical, financial, and legal ideas that seemed to constantly bounce around his head. As part of his intellectual quest, Frank went to a library one day in his native California and found the works of Darwin stretching before him. Searching for a compendium so that he could research some key words, he looked for the word "cooperation" and could not find it. Was it possible, thought Frank, that Darwin was so fixated on the competitive nature of the universe that he had neglected to see the endless examples of cooperation that were all around him? Perhaps Darwin had no need for cooperation to make his case, so simply left it out as a distraction? Or perhaps he had used similar words, and indeed had a strong sense of the cooperative nature of the universe, as a recent film suggests?[12] Whatever the case, Frank saw an opportunity to merge Darwinian competition with cooperation, and so came up with *co-opetition*. As soon as he did that, many things made sense to him.

Frank came to see the universe as, to use an awkward but useful word, *endlessly co-opetitive*. From human life to the animal kingdom to the plant world, he saw co-opetition in action everywhere he looked. He did not have to go far to see this in action in nature: just a short trip up the California coast, Frank could visit the Año Nuevo state park and its elephant seals. During mating season, a fierce battle wages between the males for the one dominant position which will be available that year. This is not some handsome and charming male peacock dance in front of the females; some fights are to the death, and in true Darwinian style, a winner emerges who will mate with *all the females*. But something else extraordinary happens: *the defeated males form a circle around the female harem and the dominant male*, which serves to keep out any further male competitors. The former competitors have become servants; *competition, sometimes to the death, has become cooperation.* In the end, with this stroke of natural genius, the strongest pups are born and the cycle goes on from there. Would it not be nice to have this genetic "on-off competition switch" implanted in some of our more ultra-competitive work colleagues?

Nature seems to love cooperation as much as it loves competition. Some birds such as Pelicans fly in formation—that familiar "V" shape we see with geese and ducks as well. Why do they do this? Thanks to endless millennia of trial and error the genius of nature has found a way to conserve energy and derive other benefits by flying this way:

> The first and most accepted [theory] is that the flight formation plays an aerodynamic role: each individual makes an upwash behind its wing tips offering to those behind it an extra lift. The other theory sustains that the flight in a slightly skewed position relative to the previous bird permits an unimpaired vision ... [when tested by researchers] the results showed that both theories hold true.[13]

It seems that leaders also regularly change places with those at the end of the "V," so that they too can benefit from the energy conservation, which being a leader does not provide. Maybe this is a model for some of our burned-out CEOs!

Seagulls might fight noisily during the day about various territorial issues and over pieces of food (competition) but at the end of the day they line up peacefully on the beach, facing into the breeze, as if they had never said a bad "word" to each other! Dolphins fish in teams, "herding" fish so that they can be easily eaten by the group. Pilot fish eat the parasites that plague much larger fish, thereby giving themselves a meal and enabling the fish to survive without being slowly eaten alive by the parasites. Conveniently, the large fish give the pilot fish a pass when it comes to selecting their seafood menu for the day. Similarly, flowers compete for the attention of bees with color and fragrance, but a solitary flower growing by itself might not be so successful; flowers have adapted to grow together or in large numbers on one plant. Bees cannot resist that!

While these behaviors may have been random events at the earliest stages of their development, they must have proven so useful that natural selection favored those creatures and plants that exhibited them. Nature does not settle on a "solution" unless it has been thoroughly tested and adds value. Since our list of both competitive and cooperative behaviors in nature could be almost endless, one thing becomes clear: *competition plus cooperation means survival.*

Our biggest and best businesses often practice co-opetition: Microsoft and Apple have been fierce competitors for years; they both offer the fundamental building block that makes personal (and other) computers run, the operating system. Yet they are also cooperators: Microsoft makes its Office productivity software for Apple computers, and has done for many years. Apple in turn is one of the biggest software contributors to users of Microsoft's Windows operating system, thanks to the popularity of Apple's iTunes multimedia software.[14]

In 1997, at a very difficult time for Apple, Microsoft (MS) and Apple made a deal to work together and MS invested $150 million in Apple. If we listen to what Steve Jobs of Apple said on the day of that announcement, we hear him talking with great humility as he moves his company toward a more cooperative stance with its former arch competitor and new partner:

> If we want to move forward and see Apple healthy and prospering again, we have to let go of a few things here. We have to let go of this notion that for Apple to win, Microsoft has to lose ... And if others are going to help us that's great, because we need all the help we can get ... So I think that is a very important perspective. If we want Microsoft Office on the Mac, we better treat the company that puts it out with a little bit of gratitude; we like their software. So, the era of setting this up as a competition between Apple and Microsoft is over as far as I'm concerned. This is about getting Apple healthy.[15]

Like the seagulls, these companies have squabbled from time to time, especially in the early years when they were both hungry upstarts, before they both became enormously successful and profitable. They have even sued each other.[16] Now they are settled down into a pleasant form of co-opetition and their billionaire founders even playfully teased each other from time to time.[17,18]

Think about your local grocery store: on its shelves you might have a brand name of cornflakes or coffee but right next to it is a cheaper version of the same thing with the "private label" of the store chain on it. Sometimes the store makes its own cornflakes or coffee and so competes with the brand names even while selling both on the same shelf (cooperation). Yet quite often these private label brands are manufactured by the very brand against which the private label product is competing. So the brand is competing with itself while cooperating with the store to give customers more choice. *This is co-opetition in action.* The store sells the brand name to those for whom this is important, and the cheaper version to those who feel that all corn flakes are the same. The manufacturer and the store both win, and so does the consumer.

Even the Beatles exhibited co-opetition: Paul McCartney and John Lennon competed fiercely as to song writing. The "winner" got to be the lead singer on his song, of course. At the same time they were so cooperative with each other that

> To the public, Lennon and McCartney famously declared themselves a fused pair. As soon as they began to write together, they decided to share credit regardless of individual contribution.[19]

Their relationship of both competing and cooperating was described by their celebrated recording manager, George (now Sir George) Martin as "tension between the two of them [which] made for the bond."[20]

A dedicated fan of capitalism and all its benefits, and a political viewpoint definitely right of center, with strong emphasis on individual freedom and responsibility, Frank Asaro did not approach the idea of co-opetition from a liberal perspective. Having studied Adam Smith and Ayn Rand, he is one of those Americans (of which there are many) for whom the word "socialism" makes his hair stand on end. Nonetheless, he realized that "co-opetition" was *aligned with how he felt inside*, with how he wanted the business world to function. He believed that we could follow our natural drives to strive and succeed (à la Ayn Rand), while still cooperating with each other (not like Ayn Rand, who appears to have been something of a tyrant![21]) This view was reinforced for him when he found some of his *most successful law clients* pushing hard to negotiate deals, but often, as he put it, "leaving something on the table" for the other party rather than "wiping them out." This created goodwill, which came back to those clients many times over, as former competitors became clients or partners in cases, for example. Those who did not fall into those categories remained competitors, as they had been before; this ensured, in its own small way, that Frank's clients would be kept on their toes. Had they "wiped everyone out," this would not be the case. Co-opetition therefore gives us an interesting paradox: *by injecting cooperation into the mix, it ensures a competitive environment, going forward.*

### Balance: Good enough for the universe, and our organizations

Co-opetition suggests that life is a *balance* between the drive to compete and the need to cooperate. When these are balanced, evolution pushes relentlessly forward and survival is optimized. As humans we should understand the concept of balance quite well, since we are beneficiaries of countless balancing acts performed for us, day and night.

*Balance as the basis of life*

Most people hardly give a moment's thought to how their body works, since (fortunately for us) nearly everything is on autopilot, except for the fulfillment of basic needs for shelter, food, elimination and reproduction, which require a little assistance! The delicate balancing acts continually going on inside the human body, though, are extraordinary. For example, our blood has to balance itself between being thin enough to go everywhere in our bodies, even into the smallest vessel, but thick enough that it can coagulate; this is enormously complex, involving at least 50 processes, all of which must "go right."[22] We become a little more aware of this if we consider things we ingest: take the right amount of Vitamin E and we will benefit from its antioxidant properties. Take too much and we will endanger ourselves. Eat a small number of Brazil nuts and enjoy big nutritional benefits; eat too many and we will suffer the effects of too much selenium.

*Balance and the human condition*

One would think that as beings supremely dependent on balance just to stay alive, we would be pre-programmed enough to ensure this in that part of our lives that is not automatic, to live in a balanced state that optimizes our life's possibilities. But clearly we forget to do this: some of us eat too much, or drink too much, or take drugs that harm our internal chemistry, some of us smoke—and the imbalance represented by these actions brings us to diabetes, alcoholism, drug addiction and cancer.

Which animal lives like this? It seems that only man does. Our "advanced" brains allow us such a range of choices that we can *choose to be out of balance*. If we look at this *apparently* dysfunctional, unbalanced behavior in isolation it might not make sense; but from another perspective, maybe it does. To explain this, *imagine that a lot of what we humans do is an attempt to be in balance.* Why would we do this? Because we experience balance as a sense of "ease," and ease is effortless and pleasurable. The dysfunctional behavior we see, according to this theory, *is merely an attempt to return to this state of ease*, sometimes called *homeostasis*. Of course, this is not the only reason that people eat too much of the wrong things: for example, the scientists of major food makers have ingeniously invented and refined things that *do not exist in that state in nature*, such as high fructose corn syrup. These appeal to deep desires in the body for sugars and fats, and many become addicted. So much for a *"balanced"* diet, when one comes to crave fat laden foods, whether we call them chips, crisps, "French fries" or hamburgers.

But let's go back to our ego-driven boss from hell to look at the argument that even she might be trying to be *in balance*. She does not enjoy living this way; in fact she is a very unhappy, person, "ill at ease." Her life is on a knife-edge because at any moment she can fall from her perch, which is supported by various external props that keep her suspended there. She must be constantly vigilant. This person did not have a happy childhood and developed this ego-based *persona* to try and feel better about herself. Anyone near her can tell this is not working, but she has been doing it so long it is like second nature to her. Letting it go would be experienced as a catastrophe. To her, though, this is an attempt at feeling good about herself, feeling at "ease," being liked by others, being "good enough." *It is an attempt to bring the balance back*, which she lost many years before when she stopped feeling any natural and "easy" sense of well-being. Unfortunately, this is a misguided "rebalancing act;" a far better alternative would be to get some professional help and begin a true healing process that brings her back to her real self.

Smoking is similar: the addicted smoker feels a sense of "ease" with each puff. Thanks to chemicals similar to those stimulated in the brain by some antidepressants, cigarettes continue to sell well around the world, despite their known dangers. They provide "ease" to people, and they help them feel more balanced.[23]

Balance is therefore fundamental to life, both from a physical and psychological perspective. It is essential to both individuals and groups such as organizations. *Balance is central to any successful organizational culture.* When we ignore it, things can go very, very wrong.

## Co-opetition, balance and Ayn Rand

We put the phrase *"Balancing Me and We"* in the title of this book to anchor our belief that a shift in this direction is central to a successful work culture for the future. We have discussed the many reasons why this is so, and given evidence from the Crash as to the consequences of an imbalance toward the "me" orientation. Nonetheless, we are mindful of the popularity of books like Ayn Rand's *Atlas Shrugged*, which appears to be experiencing a mini-sales boom, going from an average of 70,000 copies a year in the 1980s to an extraordinary 300,000 in the first half of 2009 alone.[24] Are we swimming against this tide? Political gurus with a tendency to the right are excited to point out that there is a strong correlation between President Obama being in power and *Atlas Shrugged* sales.[25] A push back from *"Obamanomics"* may not be the only reason for this surge in popularity: this period also coincides with the Crash and its after-effects, some of which preceded this President.

Ayn Rand's popularity would indicate that, at least in some section of the world's business community, her values of "self-interest"[26] and against government involvement in capitalism are resonating strongly. This is unsurprising if one takes a rather one-sided view that *only government* was involved in the

Crash, which we do not. We see Wall Street's role as being very clear and of equal culpability, as we have tried to demonstrate in these pages. Rand and her passionate followers seem to have had a bit of a blind spot about the dark side of capitalism, and especially its ability to "self-correct." Given the way that Wall Street went cap in hand to the government to be bailed out in the Crash, this seems to have shown itself to be a too-optimistic prediction. Having said that, we do believe that Rand's work does carry an important and valuable message:

> Capitalism, not some heavy-handed system of social engineering and enforced equality, is the way forward, the way to bring out the natural drive of humans to create and to prosper.

Where we part company is that, while we understand and appreciate the idea of self-sufficiency and personal responsibility, we do not buy into the idea that self-interest and the achievement of one's own personal happiness is the highest moral standing that exists. Too much imbalance in that direction is what got us in the mess from which we are only now extricating ourselves. Did the Goldman Sachs traders who were accused by the government of deceiving their customer read Rand and think that as long as they were happy and getting well paid they were at the highest moral level? Is there not a danger of this when one fully subscribes to that philosophy?

In any case, we see moral value elsewhere than self-interest: is an entrepreneur running a large and successful business, *and doing so by taking good care of her workers*, not also someone in high moral standing? We believe she is. Does she have to run this business only for her "self interest," squeezing out every drop for herself and "to hell with everyone else"? Her chances of survival might be much less if she were. Capitalism does not have to involve only self-interest (competition); just like the universe itself, capitalism thrives when cooperation is present, as we have seen. Cooperation with one's workers, with all benefiting from the resulting success of the organization, is surely a high moral state to reach. So while there is a portion of the business community that has taken to following Rand and believing she has all the answers, we suggest taking her best ideas, but avoiding her worst ones. In doing so, we stick by our assertion that there needs to be a move away from Rand-style self-interest, not to socialism or any form of increased government control, but to a more *conscious form of capitalism*. That begins with a culture that will support it.

In discussing what factors must be considered in the sustainable, high engagement work culture, we have listed our set of requirements and then placed a lot of emphasis on *balance*; in particular, but by no means limited to, the balance between competition and cooperation. These will be our foundations as we move to build our vision of an organizational culture that really works. We know this because, as we shall see later, some are brave, smart and *generous* enough to be already using these ideas.

### The sustainable, high engagement work culture: How might it look? How does it work?

Our purpose now is simple: to bring together all that we have seen so far and focus this on building a better cultural model for our organizations, *one whose outcome will be high engagement*. The implementation of this is not so simple: it might require a seismic shift in an organization.

What do we need to remember in order to do this? Here is a reminder:

- We need to remember first and foremost that engagement is about *building an emotional connection*. This has very significant consequences for what need to do.
- We need to remember that engagement is something our people will choose to do, *not something we can make them do*. It is our job to create the environment that is so attractive to them that engagement will be something they gladly and easily do. We want them to be excited to come to work!

To see the flow of how a culture is built, let's go back to our pyramid:

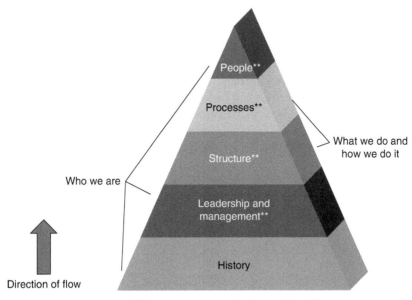

*Chart 4.1*  Building the high engagement culture

Given that we cannot change the organization's history, our pyramid gives us four levers we can use to change, improve or create a new high engagement culture:

- Leadership and management, their values, skills and their ability to work with people.
- The structure of our organization.
- All the formal and informal processes we create and use to achieve our mission. This includes the types of relationships that are formed between managers and workers and between workers themselves; how we pay people, how and what we communicate, how we manage performance; in other words *how we treat our people* in those many formal and informal contacts, which they have with the organization day by day.
- Our people: their talents, values, behavior, and so on.

If we are to build a culture that works, we need to find a way to look at all the previous points—*who we are as individuals and as an organization, and at all that we do*—and filter this through our "requirements" so that only the best parts remain. This is best understood with a short story about a job one of us had, just briefly, and a long time ago:

> In the west of England there was a famous chocolate factory, only recently closed, which made the chocolate bars that the Brits (along with others they had influenced around the world with their sporting and eating habits) craved. One of their best-known products was the Picnic bar, a simple yet totally addictive mix of peanuts covered with milk chocolate. When we signed on to a summer job there, we were put on Picnic production, and being the newest hire, were put in charge of peanut shelling. This involved shaking a large sieve with partially shelled peanuts until only the peanuts remained. Why this had not been assigned to a machine, was beyond our knowledge and very modest pay grade, but it had not. After four hours of shaking this sieve, we were asked if we could start early the next morning, at 7:00 a.m. instead of 8:00 so that the team could meet its incentive bonus. Having agreed, we asked for an early lunch and never came back. About two months later, a check for five shillings appeared in the mail for our four hours of shaking, minus all social security and other tax deductions. We never ate another Picnic bar.

We are asking you to shake out your *individual and organizational beliefs, values and practices* to remove all the pieces of shell and leave only the best material! But don't just do it for four hours.

We will make it easy: by creating a virtual "sieve" we call the **BEST** *test*.

**Applying *BEST practices* and the *BEST test***

In order to create the high engagement culture, our guide will be all of the requirements that we have listed earlier in this chapter, which (quite by coincidence!) can be summarized with the very convenient acronym ***BEST***:

**B**alanced
**E**ngagement-friendly
**S**ustainable
**T**rackable

> Most of our requirements fit into one or more of the BEST categories. The categories also support each other, in that balance creates greater sustainability and engagement-friendliness; tracking things means that we know where we are starting from and whether we are reaching our cultural and engagement goals, all of which means we can sustain our efforts and are more likely to be successful.

Imagine an organization where everything is run through the ***BEST*** *test*: we believe it would be a place where high engagement is not only possible but *significantly more probable*. ***BEST*** gives us a road map and means:

- That we try to stay *appropriately* balanced[27] across all parts of our organization: for example, we keep the ego firmly under control in whatever we do by balancing "me" and "we." We balance competition and cooperation so that we have healthy doses of each.
- That we do not permit short-term focused behavior, which places the longer term in jeopardy, *thereby increasing our chances of sustainability*. Ethical behavior belongs in the same category; clearly, unethical behavior is *unsustainable* as well as negative for worker *engagement* (see further).
- That we focus at all times on whether what we do will move us closer to an *engagement-friendly environment*. This means, for example:
  o That we focus on *fairness factors* such as *equality of opportunity but not outcomes*, on performance and not just longevity.
  o That we are mindful of open and honest communications, upwards, downwards and sideways.
  o That we act *ethically* both internally with our people and with all our external stakeholders such as customers and suppliers.
  o That we apply our people-oriented *values* to all that we do.
- That we have a *means to track* how we are doing and what we need to change along the way. Often this will involve a survey, the best method by far for finding out what people feel in an organization, in anything but the smallest organizations, *and even then*.

*With **BEST*** and its four easy focus points as our guide, we can proceed to examine our work cultures from the ground up, starting with something extremely important, *the emotional connection.*

### Leadership: Consequences of engagement as an emotional connection

This is the first stop because it is fundamental. Since worker engagement is an emotional connection, the consequences are *that individuals in leadership positions who are not emotionally skilled and self-knowledgeable will be hard-pressed to lead an organization toward the high engagement culture.* Similarly, people who occupy positions of management, whether at the first line or higher, will have a difficult time making any *existing high engagement culture come alive* with what they do. For this reason, leaders and managers need to take personal responsibility for something that will be central to whether a culture of *sustainable high engagement* can take root in their organizations. To do this they must look inside themselves, honestly and openly. As the justifiably celebrated management Peter Drucker said: one must *"Manage Oneself"*![28]

Fortunately there are signs that green shoots are coming up in the area of emotional knowledge and skills for managers. US business schools such as Columbia, UC Berkeley's Haas and Stanford are offering such classes as *"Touchy-Feely"*[29] (Stanford), and ones that focus on reining in what we have discussed here as ego-based behavior (Berkeley).[30] While these are good signs, they come into an environment in which such things have not always been well accepted by the students who are now learning them in greater numbers. In a 2007 study of 373 business schools by researchers at DePaul University, there was a clear demonstration that, *at that time*, there was a long way to go in the B-School world of emotional knowledge.

The study asked some 8600 managers and 118 deans of B-schools about these so-called soft skills, which are taught in such schools. The results showed that

- Managers believe that decision-making and managing "human capital" are two of the most important part of their jobs, and both require significant knowledge in the "soft skills;" yet these subjects were found to be covered in only 13% and 10% of required courses, respectively, at the 373 B-schools studied.[31]
- According to the deans surveyed, however, B-school students have a quite different perspective and are much less "soft-skill" oriented than those who are already in the job of manager. Since student demand partly drives curriculum, this leads one of the study authors to say: "It tells the story that perhaps the customer is not always right."[32]

Perhaps the Crash will focus some students' attention on the fact that the "softer" skills might have helped us avoid at least some of the problems we have discussed, and that some *"EQ"* might be something worth having as much as IQ. We hope this is true; our future worker engagement levels depend on how seriously this is taken by the next generation of leaders.

*Building from the ground up: Leaders, check your EQ!*

We are referring here to *emotional intelligence*, a field that has been around since the late 1990s and been boosted by such books as the 1996 *Emotional Intelligence*[33] and more recent offerings.[34] EQ is very different to, and not cor-related to IQ! *Yet it is EQ and not IQ, which is the main determinant of success in business and life.* The reason we stress it here is that leadership is very crucial to everything that happens in the organization, and to its values and culture, yet so many leaders do not seem to understand that they have responsibility to be intelligent in this area, which means EQ-smart and not just IQ-smart. EQ gives people the capability to handle their emotions, understand the emotions of others and handle them too. It is the building block for relationships, both inside and outside the workplace. EQ is a major tool for communicators, which leaders are—or should be—most of the time. *All this is essential in building the high engagement culture.*

Now here is the most surprising—and shocking—thing of all: *CEOs score poorly on EQ, especially in the US*, where many have been tested. Interestingly, in China, top-level managers do much better. Given the many benefits that accrue from this, and the essential nature of EQ for the high engagement cul-ture, leaders everywhere need to make it a top priority to

- Identify their own EQ levels
- Improve their understanding of themselves, their emotions and how all this affects how they do their job

This does not mean that they have to buy a particular book or follow a particu-lar methodology. There are many paths to higher EQ, just as there are many paths to whatever we might call the "higher power." There are seminars on this and related subjects everywhere, there are therapists who can help, study groups and, of course, many books.

Identifying and improving one's EQ passes the **BEST** test in several ways:

- Enhancing EQ allows a person to become more balanced emotionally and not be a victim of his or her emotions; this is a critical skill for managers to master.
- It also means that an individual can balance IQ with EQ instead of having a lopsided (and far less valuable, performance-wise) IQ-bias. Knowledge is power, but one-sided knowledge, *which leaves out emotional understanding*, is only half that power.

- A higher EQ means much more *self-awareness* and that is an antidote to ego-istic behavior. The ego prefers that as little light as possible be shone on its activities. The more awareness, the more ego will melt under its light.
- Learning about one's emotions and those of others makes a person more free of baggage from the past; it improves health, and so adds to the individual's personal sustainability and that of their personal relationships at work and at home.
- A high EQ manager, armed with self-knowledge and not just driven by her emotions, will be much better at forming the personal relationships that are the bedrock of worker engagement. The same is true of a higher EQ indi-vidual contributor, who will be much easier to work with, and take far less time to "manage."
- Tracking one's EQ is possible through various widely available tests and is a fun and useful thing to do when one embarks on this path. Tracking the *effects* of improving one's EQ is a common feature of many engagement surveys and 360 reviews.

Any investment in this will be of huge benefit, and not just at work. How can an organization have a high engagement culture if its leaders are low in EQ? We think it is much less likely. After all, since *engagement is all about emo-tion*, why not learn as much as one can about that? That is an inner journey worth making: *a manager who takes that journey benefits both herself and her organization.*

### Building from the ground up: Values

*Values*: there may be no more important word in this book apart from *engage-ment*, because values will drive everything that comes after them, including engagement. There is no one set of values that applies to all organizations, because no organization has your history, leaders, people, position in the mar-ket, mission and vision. Only you have this mix and only you can decide what values are truly important for you going forward. If you run a coal mine, an automobile company or an insurance company, some of your values will over-lap and some will not. The coal mine will emphasize safety and the insurance company, financial security; both should emphasize people orientation. This is why the discussion has to include the *mission and the vision*, because of the alignment necessary between those and values.

Values are not always easy to identify, and they also change over time; many organizations with which we have worked and read about have spent from a day to months or much more discussing this and come up with a list of values and a statement that brings them all together. This is hardly surprising because you are getting to the core of why you exist, what it is you want to achieve *and how*; a lot of people have opinions about this, although not all organizations listen as much as the London Business School (LBS). The Dean of LBS, Sir Andrew Likierman, recently visited this subject for his own organization, with something called The Values Project:

> This has been to identify *what makes us different from other business schools, what we are seeking to do as a school.* We have seven or eight groups of stakeholders here [such as alumni, governing Board, students] and we talked to the stakeholders about how they saw us as an institution and what they felt we stood for.[35]

(emphasis added)

LBS spent no less than *18 months* on this project. As part of this effort, Sir Andrew and his stakeholders added the global nature of LBS as part of its values and culture. Clearly, all of this will drive the direction and behavior of LBS into the future; such is the power of values.

Because of the uniqueness of this step, we cannot tell you what to emphasize. What we have done is give you some examples: we have seen what we feel to be an excellent values statement, that of Hilti. It is simple and clear, and it can be easily communicated to all levels of people in the organization. This should be your goal too. We have also seen the comprehensive and extremely inclusive efforts of London Business School. If you need inspiration, go to the web sites of companies or nonprofits you admire and see if they talk about values and culture; often they do, as we saw with Google. This is a crucial first step; everything you do will flow from this and can and should be checked against it.

*Values can make or break an organization*

One should never underestimate the power of values. Don't just take our word for it: in 1985 Apple's Board of directors forced out founder Steve Jobs, who did not return until 1997. John Sculley, a former executive of Pepsi took over as CEO from 1985, and Jobs' view of his performance and what he did to Apple was scathing in the extreme, but totally focused on the kinds of values we have talked about in this book. Here is what Jobs said:

> John Sculley ruined Apple and he ruined it *by bringing a set of values to the top of Apple* which were corrupt and corrupted some of the top people who were there, drove out some of the ones who were not corruptible, and brought in more corrupt ones and paid themselves collectively tens of millions of dollars and cared more about their own glory and wealth than they did about what built Apple in the first place—which was making great computers for people to use.[36]

(emphasis added)

*Better no stated values than unlived ones*

Over the years in which we have assisted clients with the development of value statements and the measurement of those values within their organizations, one thing has become patently clear: *it is far, far better to have no value statement of any kind, anywhere, than one which is not lived by the organization.* If the values are not lived, the statement on the organization's web site or in its annual report will be greeted by employees with (internally felt and/or externally expressed) derision. What is worse than being reminded, day by day, of hypocrisy?

We are not talking here about when an organization has had a big change and a new CEO has come in to "turn things around." Sometimes then values can be stated *as goals*, not as actuality, until there is proof they really are talking hold. The gap between stated and lived values was covered in the 2009 UK government "MacLeod Report" on *Engaging for Success*:[37]

> Where there is a gap between the two, the size of the gap is reflected in the degree of distrust within the organisation; if the gap is closed, high levels of trust usually result.

We appreciate the use of this word "trust." Trust is part of the bedrock of worker engagement. Without trust, how can one even imagine an engaged workforce? Yes, workers can be engaged in their individual jobs even if they do not trust the organization, but a whole part of engagement is missing. Our experience has been that, over time, this lack of trust in the larger organization will undermine even an enthusiastic feeling toward one's own job.

*Changing values*

Change (good or bad) can happen when a leader arrives with a new set of values and immediately starts to treat people differently based on them. Typically, that leader also brings in executives who are "a good fit;" this means they fit his or her values, among other things. Mid-level management is also selected according to written or nonwritten values and beliefs.

Change in this area never happens overnight. Values take time to build in the hearts and minds of workers. They will take a "wait and see" attitude when someone new comes in, whether at the top of the organization or to lead their team. They will test those values in various ways to find out if the organization is "walking the talk" or not, and whether the values are consistently applied and *enforced*.

*Tracking and enforcing values*

One of us once had a client whose CEO was quite religious; he made quite stringent demands on his top echelon, that they also be religiously active and *never, ever* do something that would betray the values of that religion. This was a little hard for some of these individuals, who found that violation of the values was a terminal disease, as far as their job was concerned. However, it was not unexpected, and in fact their apparent adherence to the organization's values during the hiring process was clearly part of their reason for being there. We are not advocating this, merely demonstrating the power of values and some of the ways those values are *enforced*. Now we realize that the word "enforce" is quite an unexpected one in the context of what is seen as a "softer" side of the organization, its values. Yet, values do need to be enforced, the same way that we rely on referees and judges in sports. Without enforcement, the values will die and baser human instincts might fill that gap. Vigilance is key here, as is consistency and fairness. We are always impressed by clients who put values so much front and center that they will let even star performers go, who violate core values. This sends a powerful message: *"we will do whatever it takes to live as we have stated; no one person is more important to us that our organization's values."* If the stars are allowed to "get away with it" because they "deliver results," values will become eroded. *Enforcement therefore means that values become sustainable.*

Key here is whether and how the organization *measures whether it is living up to its stated values*. The best practices we have seen here involve using survey research to make this measurement. Bumping into people in an elevator and asking them about this does not qualify as a scientific piece of research. Many organizations now survey their employees, but not all actually state the values in the questionnaire and ask if the employee believes that that is the way things are. Simple questions can add this powerful feature to your survey. We recognize that this is not always possible when one is "locked in" to a standardized engagement survey, for example, with no possibility of customization, but if such a feature is available, we recommend using it. Values can be approached directly or indirectly. A typical *direct question* might look like this:

**Q: To what extent do you believe the following "values" are *lived* in [your organization name]?**

**Teamwork**

| Little Extent | 1 | 2 | 3 | 4 | 5 | Great Extent |
|---|---|---|---|---|---|---|

**Respect for people**

| Little Extent | 1 | 2 | 3 | 4 | 5 | Great Extent |
|---|---|---|---|---|---|---|

**Customer focus**

| Little Extent | 1 | 2 | 3 | 4 | 5 | Great Extent |
|---|---|---|---|---|---|---|

**Innovation**

| Little Extent | 1 | 2 | 3 | 4 | 5 | Great Extent |
|---|---|---|---|---|---|---|

Alternatively, you can approach values slightly more indirectly, perhaps with a question that lists various values, *including yours*, and asks *which, if any*, are practiced in your organization.[38] We promise you, you might be shocked by the results, as many of our clients have been. Like much in life, values are easier said than done. At least then you will be dealing with reality and not fantasy.

### High engagement values

Some values are more "valuable" than others. Those that are valuable state clearly what the organization believes in and what it expects from its workforce and suppliers, how it plans to treat its workers, customers and so on. As to which values are most supportive of an engaging environment to which employees will be more likely to commit and give their best, this is not complicated. Values that respect people and, *when lived*, bring out the best in them will achieve this goal. It is here that organizations can make clear, as Hilti does with its *teamwork* value, that "we" is more important than "me" and in doing so can underscore what we believe to be *the core building block for an engaged workforce*.

Of course, no organization is going to openly state values that do not respect people, but they may forget (this does happen!) to make that clear. Some values are not stated because that organization has never bothered to do that; in other cases the actual, lived values are so bad, no one would ever dare state them, except in a confidential survey.

### Hiring and promoting for values and culture

Skilled recruiters and hiring managers do this instinctively. Great organizations have been doing it for some time. There is a good reason for hiring for values and cultural "fit," and that is the cost of short term employment and quick "divorce" for those who did not end up fitting your culture, *estimated at 50% to 150% of annual salary*.[39] You might therefore find it a good idea to formalize the process of hiring with specific values and your culture in mind. Just to give you one example, in an area where we have placed a great deal of focus: you might consider giving tests for narcissism to potential hires. Better to avoid this trait from the start than to hire someone who embodies it and who becomes a burden to you and your organization, as we saw in our chapter on ego. Some good tests are out there and some are quite difficult to "game," even for an intelligent test taker. Alternatively, look for instances of "me" versus "we" in your in-depth interviews. As psychologists, though, we like tests that have been thoroughly validated and used across wide populations. They will be more accurate than subjective reactions *on certain subjects* from even skilled interviewers; but they are not a replacement for the latter, by any means.

Organizations find that hiring for a values and culture "fit" has definite benefits:

- Teams with like-minded people work better together.
- Attrition can drop dramatically (50% for some organizations) when they hire with this "fit" in mind.[40]

Be careful though, because there are pitfalls here:

- Try and avoid a "sameness," which is damaging to the organization, when too much "respect" leads to nothing being challenged, for example. Balance is, once again, key.
- Ensure that "fit" does not mean any form of discrimination, or you could be in legal trouble.[41]

*Giving your values the **BEST** test*

The example of Steve Jobs and Apple is a perfect one that shows what happens when values go out of *balance*. The organization was almost driven into the ground. Was *ego* involved? Jobs' statement is full of examples of this, where he says that those brought into Apple "cared more about their glory and wealth." As far as *sustainability*, clearly these values were not going to sustain Apple, quite the opposite. As for *tracking*, we have no data on whether Apple was tracking its culture and engagement levels at that time, such that what Jobs described would have set off code red alerts on their tracking system (e.g., an employee survey). Whatever the case, we do believe strongly that tracking of values is vital for a healthy organizational culture, in the same way that a yearly health checkup is good for an individual.

## Applying *BEST practices* to all that you do. 1: Structure of your organization

Have you ever changed the structure of your organization and seen morale or engagement go up or down? It happens all the time. Sometimes layers are added, and of course peoples' pride gets bruised when they are one level further away from the top, but we are not just talking about that. The structure has many more effects on the culture and can actually increase morale and the possibilities of worker engagement. Let's look at an example:

*Delayering* is a common practice and for good reason; more in the organization become "closer to the customer." Decisions do not have to be passed through so many people and levels, and are made faster. People receive more responsibility by not having someone above them to second-guess and bless their decisions. Communications flow better, there is no "sponge" above to soak up information, perhaps keeping it to themselves to maintain control. *All these things are empowering and enhance engagement; never underestimate your organization structure's effect on engagement levels!* After all, why do the new high-tech darlings like Google with their lack of organization charts seem to operate so well with such informality? Were we wrong in being so rigid all this time, with our "org charts" and top-down command and control structure? Of course we were—to a degree (we do not advocate free-for-all, like our continual reference point of football, we need some adult supervision). Still, why do millions of people work from home, not in some office with a boss breathing down their necks? Because it is cheaper (no office space to rent) *but also it is engaging to have control over one's work life.*[42] Of course, someone has to trust you to get the job done, but that is the whole point: *you decide when and how that happens, and the fact that you are trusted is even more engaging.*

If you do have an organization chart, which most do, then flipping it upside down could be a good exercise. Some have done this: many years ago the airline SAS did so. This implied that the CEO worked for *everyone "above,"* which not all CEOs might like to think. It put the customer on top, and those closest to the customer next to the top. Managers work for their teams, not the other way around. It is certainly *empowering,* and we see some organizations actually work this way, even if they may not have charts that show this. The managers at Starbucks that we have met certainly talk this way: that they work for their teams. We find this very impressive, and we believe it is one of those approaches that create the environment in which engagement flourishes. Plenty of research shows that empowerment of workers improves productivity, morale and engagement.[43] Flip the old "org chart"—in reality or *virtually in people's minds*—and see how such a radical step changes your engagement levels. Applying the **BEST** test to this, flipping the chart *rebalances* the power scales between workers and management. Although workers know that they are not running the show, the chart shows them as the most important part of the show because they are on top; the importance of their proximity to customers is highlighted and reinforced, and the fact that *people make the difference* is recognized well beyond a statement in the annual report. It is certainly *engagement-friendly,* as we have noted. We will expand on this idea further when looking at processes.

### Applying the *BEST* test to all that you do. 2: Your processes

*Finding your own **BEST** practices and internal benchmarking*

Since culture is the way you do things, you need to take all the important things you do with people in your organization and run them through the **BEST** test. Unlike other books (of which there are many) that give you a list of what to do on Monday morning to improve morale or engagement, *our goal is* *to provide you with a process with which you can create something that works best for you, not a list of what to do.* This is a fundamentally different approach based our belief that *one size does not fit all.* We want you to identify and create your own **BEST** *practices.* We can explain this better by giving you an example:

> Many organizations conduct employee surveys of morale, job satisfaction or engagement. Most do so with the help of consultants, some of whom have invested enormous sums in "norms" or comparative databases. These can be specific to an industry or a country or both. They can often be broken down by job "level" as well. Many organizations base what they do with survey data on comparisons between themselves and these norms, *which we believe to be a mistake.* The reason is that there are often huge differences between the normative databases, even for the same industry and the same time frame. A recent example is whether engagement went down after the 2008 Crash; some say it did and others say it did not, and these are big, prestigious firms we are talking about![44]
>
> So not only is data from other organizations unreliable, you need to remember that it is based on those organizations' cultures, which is in turn based on their values, beliefs, history, etc. *None of which is yours.*

The lesson is that you should not base your work culture just on a list of what others do outside of your organization, even others who have been very successful. This is advice a good therapist gives individuals too: be who *you* are, not a copy of others. This is not to say that other organizations don't have good ideas you can use or (better) adapt, with a big caveat: *they do not have your culture, and that is a major issue.* What worked for them and their unique circumstances might not work for you. Finding out what *you* do best is an important exercise; we have accomplished this with many organizations by analyzing their worker survey data and seeing which units excel, both from the point of view of engagement and also performance. For example, it is smart to blend in other data such as customer satisfaction, so you can correlate this with engagement and find out which engagement factors and management practices go with highly satisfied customers *in your organization.* This is what one of us did for Hilti, and which had a huge payoff for that company.[45] Another true-life example is that of a hospital system in which one accident/emergency department (A&E or ER) scored far higher on morale than another in the same system, with equally awful external conditions (crime, number and seriousness of injuries, etc.) How could one do so well and the other so poorly? We asked the same question of the poorly performing ER's manager, whom the CEO then dispatched to see exactly what was being done to make the first ER so people-friendly, despite dealing with similar conditions. Having the internal benchmark and best practice available within the organization made the poor-performing ER manager's task much easier, and his defense that such performance was not possible in his circumstances without merit.

Mining internal data for your own best practices, creating internal bench-marks from this, *balancing* all this with the best that is being done outside your organization, and putting your own processes through the **BEST** *test* are smart things to do. Here are some of the areas you might look at as you keep the **BEST** factors in mind:

- *Balance between stakeholders*
  We refer here to owners (whether individuals, families or public shareholders), workers/employees, customers, suppliers, the larger community, etc. All are invested in, and dependent on, the success of the organization. The question is how to balance resources given to each. For example, how much does a family take out of a small business they own, and how much do they reinvest for capital improvements, workers salaries, training and benefits, and so on. *This balance can make a huge difference in morale and engagement levels, customer satisfaction, etc.*
  - Our requirement that all must "win" is a *critical* component in the balance here. For example, no culture that supports customers being treated badly is sustainable, even though companies like Enron were spectacularly "successful" until they crashed in flames and their utter contempt for customers was revealed.[46]
  - Balance in community involvement versus shareholder interests: It is not always cheap to be involved in the communities one serves. Some companies pay a percentage of their profits to community organizations, which appear to take away from shareholders. This balance is a fine one, but the payoff in goodwill over time can be substantial, and can benefit shareholders in return. This is a much bigger issue, one that also includes *corporate social responsibility*, which we will explore in Chapter 6.
- *Management style 1: Balance of power, control versus self-direction*
  - This means more than how you are structured, although that is an important part (see previous). Structure can hide how things *actually work* as opposed to how they work on paper. So structural changes are not required to delegate decisions and activities, but that helps: a rigid hierarchical structure on paper is more likely to generate rigidity in practice. Flattening the structure means that power-hungry managers no longer have the "org chart" as an excuse for their behavior. Of course, that does not solve the psychological problem from which some suffer: *the need for control.* Workplace trends also play a role: pity the "control-freak" manager who finds his organization moving toward flexible work hours and working from home! These powerful trends are doing a lot to loosen control no matter who is in the management positions.

○ Balance of power is key to *engagement* because the latter is partly driven by how much power and control people have. This is *one* of the main reasons why engagement and morale scores rise as one moves "up" the organization: the correlation with control. Having said that, great leaders and managers possessing some humility and unselfishness gladly delegate to others, knowing that this lightens their own load and empowers their people, two huge benefits. *No smart worker is going to engage in an organization where she is not trusted with appropriate decisions and activities, without being micro-managed.* One movement we have seen in recent years in the idea of *manager as "servant" rather than "master"*,[47] although this is not without controversy especially when applied to top leaders.[48] Some might be shocked at the word "servant," bringing to mind images of the British TV series *Downton Abbey*, and all that that implies. To those who feel that way, we offer more appealing words for managers such as *supporter, facilitator, coach*, etc. while still holding on to the idea that this view of the manager's job (*especially those at mid and first level, but also at the very top*) is to *serve his or her people.* This is an interesting phenomenon because it dovetails with our idea above of flipping the organizational chart, even if only virtually. All, of course, serve the (internal or external) customer, in case anyone should forget why they are there.

○ There can be resistance to this: delegation means giving up power, and we know how some people hate that. This is a psychological issue as much as anything else; some managers, even at the very top, have to have control dragged out of their hands before they let go. So not everyone will want to go along with this approach. The ego hates the idea that a manager should serve anyone: after all, hasn't it worked and waited for years to get to this position where it can Lord it over people and "call the shots"? The best managers know all about this, though, and do it intuitively. They know that they will bring out the best in their people when they serve them. They know that there is no loss in "status" in serving people, whether those in their team or customers. *They know it is not demeaning to serve.* The irony is that there is a *gain in status* when the survey comes out and shows that their team is way ahead in engagement. Letting go of control means a new kind of power emerges: *the power of their people.* Since control is a major engagement issue, and engagement is correlated with how much control has been delegated, this is an important area to examine. *Track* it easily with your survey: you will see that managers who delegate and empower will have more engaged people working "*with*" (not "*for*") them. Aside from tracking, delegation and manager-as-servant passes the **BEST** test with flying colors: it is a major rebalancing exercise between management and workers, is highly engagement-friendly and creates a more sustainable work environment by moving an organization away from a *command and control culture* that burns people out and drives them away.

- *Management style 2: Balance between being "tough" or "tender"*
  - ○ Do your managers fire people quickly if they do not perform? Or do they bend over backwards to look at every mitigating circumstance, giving them the "benefit of the doubt"? Do they set tough goals for people to reach and then hold them 100% accountable? Do they allow people to go against the values you state as core to your organization's culture, with no real consequences? Or do they crack down as soon as those values are violated? *Track this by looking at your survey data for signs of what management style is used, and see what the overall result is for engagement of your workers who are in that person's team.* Engaged workers respond to fairness and consistency of application (when fair, not when unfair!). They respond favorably to being held accountable, but not in a totally rigid way. We are human and sometimes things happen, like when a child becomes sick and we miss a goal. *There is plenty of room for compassion in the high engagement workplace. Balance* comes from knowing where to draw the line in the application of this, before it becomes exploited and damages the team's sense of fairness.
- *Performance management: Engagement and values as goals*
  - ○ In the high engagement work culture, *engagement of your people becomes one of your key goals, whether you are CEO or a mid-level manager.* Adherence to values can be as well. For an individual contributor, engagement with others at work, and/or with external stakeholders, including customers, is the goal. This emphasis reinforces the importance of these things and the need to make them a constant focus. *You can track all this with surveys and 360 reviews.* Your survey will (or should) give you an overall score on engagement and you can use the values questions previously to see how individual teams are doing and look at differences between teams that are likely the result of management behavior. *Knowing how values are being lived, team by team, is a powerful piece of information.* Be careful that managers do not start to "manage to the survey." One disadvantage of a very short survey is that this is possible, just as teaching can be geared to a particular test rather than to the acquisition of knowledge about a broader field. A longer survey is impossible to "fix" in this way: if a manager finds a way to get his or her people scoring high on everything in that survey, they are most likely doing a great job, not just "gaming" the survey![49]

The idea of *tracking* an employee for adherence to the organization's values brings up the distinction between performance and behavior. In a 2009 survey of performance management conducted by the worldwide HR society SHRM, 87% of 524 HR managers reported that managing behavior was more difficult than managing performance.[50] Adherence to values is a behavioral aspect of work rather than a performance one. A job can be "performed" with little or no adherence to any core value the organization may have stated is its focus. While some will "do the right thing" automatically because of their nature, don't expect all workers to adhere to the values, unless they have been translated into expected behaviors, have been modeled by management and reinforced by everything those workers see happening in the organization. *This includes dealing swiftly and strongly with any and all violations of core values!* In this case behavior trumps performance, in that if your best "performer" is a violator of core values, your organization has a clear step to take if it wishes to count itself among the best managed and highest engagement organizations we know: *let that person go!*

Including engagement and values-based behavior as part of your performance discussions with workers is well worth the effort. It is another way that you emphasize and reinforce these things in your organization and it *balances* the emphasis that is usually made simply on the achievement of the job's goals.

- *Balance between "fun" and seriousness at work*
  - ○ It has become *de rigueur* for some technology, media and advertising companies to make their workplaces fun. The theory is that this makes for more creativity and a healthier workplace. This works well until the fun part becomes too much of a focus and crazy projects sprout up,[51] or it all becomes just too much *pressure!*[52] *Balance* is the key.
- *Balance in how people are treated (fairness)*
  - ○ Fairness has to do with much more than pay, although that is certainly a key component. Fairness touches every part of the manager-employee relationship; the *balance* challenge here is how to be fair when that means not meeting someone's expectations. The best managers know that sometimes individuals have to be disappointed so that the team can be treated fairly. Handling the inevitable conflicts that come from this is one measure of a manager's "soft" skill and emotional intelligence.
- *Balance in the ebb and flow of our workers' lives*
  - ○ Everything in the universe experiences the ebb and flow of existence, from planets to flowers to trees to human beings. We are created, we expand and then start to contract in exactly the same way that the universe itself will do, one day (but hopefully not soon). This balance is something we can use to our advantage in our organizations: we can capitalize on the expansion phase with its drive and energy (competition), while also benefiting from the contraction phase of individuals, who can share their wisdom and experience with others in mentor roles, for example (cooperation). By doing so, we increase the engagement potential of our entire workforce.

- *Communications: Top-down, bottom-up, peer to peer, social media*
  - Communications specialists have been teaching us all about this area, including the concept of "employee voice".[53] Ensuring *balance* between what comes down to people, and what comes back up from them, is crucial. People like having a "voice," knowing that they are "listened to;" engagement comes when people experience this. Why engage when no one is interested in what you have to contribute? Level or direction and content of communication are only part of the issue here: *credibility is also critical.* Workers will hardly engage when they do not believe what they are hearing. Ask them in your surveys if they do believe what they hear; you might be surprised at what they say.
  - What about the explosion in social media? What does it tell us about people and how can it be incorporated into day-to-day work life? It tells us first that human beings have an insatiable need to communicate with each other, or Facebook would never have almost 900 million members and be growing every day. Twitter is not only the medium of choice for every revolution that has taken place during the "Arab Spring" of 2011, it is also used more and more by organizations to project their brand around the world. The broad scope of this is breathtaking: just as social media bring democracy to countries that hunger for it, they also bring more democracy to the workplace![54] At work, though, there is clearly a balance issue, as discussions in HR magazines and blogs indicate. How does an organization capitalize on its workers' desire to communicate with others about work issues while maintaining some control over content? Many do not want everyone who works for them being an unofficial "voice" for the brand across the world, perhaps for good reason; at the same time, who better to project the brand but the "ambassadors" who work there? The communications specialists who work around the world have their hands full with these kinds of balancing acts; as we have seen, these experts often have a big hand in engagement efforts where they work. Hopefully they can manage social media in such a way that it:
    - *Enhances worker engagement by both informing workers and giving them a "voice."*
    - Protects the communications efforts of the organization and its investments in its brand.
- *Communications: Sustaining the culture*
  - Some communications are so important that they belong with the CEO and his or her team. This is the case with the culture itself. The very best organizations we know actively teach, discuss and reinforce the culture they have created. They do so in formal sessions in which *all must participate, every year, including Board members.* Culture stays alive first and foremost by being lived, of course, but there are often new people coming on board who need to know what it is all about. Others might need to

be reminded. Communications about the culture are never wasted: they ensure that this bedrock of your organization continues to exist and to grow. *Tracking* systems such as surveys will tell you how well it is being lived, and the annual training and communications sessions will be your chance to fill in the gaps the surveys identify for you.

- *Balance in terms of worker diversity*
  - o This is a valuable investment in many ways: ensuring balance such that the workforce, *including management*, reflects the population of the outside community (local or national, depending on size and scope), gives the organization access to a mix of talent, background and experience. This in turn counts with customers, too. Vested interests and formerly favored groups are not always happy about this. Balance here is strength, not weakness. Younger workers, with their greater than average sense of acceptance of all groups within society, be they racial, sexual orientation and so on, respond especially well to this. *Their sense of fairness and idealism makes them want to engage more with organizations that make this a priority.*

- *Balance in pressure to perform versus safety*
  - o The 2010 BP environmental disaster in the Gulf of Mexico has been heralded as an issue of balance by some: the push to complete the job of drilling and move into production, versus safety. Unfortunately, the "safety culture" seems to have taken a back seat.[55] The disaster demonstrates again just how expensive an imbalance can be, not just for one company but for society as a whole.

- *Balance between work and home life (part-time work, vacations, sick leave, parental benefits, work-at-home)*
  - o This has become a big issue for many organizations as they strive to have, for example, more women in their workforces and to satisfy the needs of those women.[56] A modern, competitive company has to offer benefits that are attractive to these workers, and flexible working conditions so that they can have balance in their lives; this is often because of national and state laws, but also because it enhances the organization's image, and the morale and engagement of those who work there. Companies like Starbucks and Whole Foods gain a lot of kudos with women for having generous benefits for part-time workers, such as working mothers. Online recruitment web sites such as Monster highlight how women can discover how women-friendly potential employers are.[57] Having more women in organizations is also valuable when they move up to management ranks: there is evidence that women managers enhance worker engagement levels![58]
  - o Another engagement-friendly situation enjoyed by some organizations is allowing people to work at home. This has been shown to be associated with high morale and engagement, and the increasing numbers of organizations using it demonstrates that it is not harmful to productivity, in fact quite the contrary.[59]

- *Balance between internal competition and cooperation; individual and team*
  - ○ Should individuals or teams compete inside the organization? Isn't it enough that they have to compete with the outside world? Will competition bring out the best in people? Or will it contribute to egos being allowed to flourish and do their damage? Where are the limits set? How do we not squash individual (or team) initiative while maintaining cohesion and cooperation across the organization and avoiding the "star culture"? We have seen the Wall Street issues here, the *individual as hero,* and we know the reaction of one firm: no more heroes. But Wall Street will have to find a way to let individuals be as good as they can be, their business depends on this. Is one degree of *balance* between individual and team, between competition and cooperation, appropriate for all organizations? No, each is unique, there is certainly not one formula for all, and only you can answer this for yours. We need to *track* how our current practices work and what effect they have on engagement. Only then will we know, for ourselves, *not for some other actual or generic organization,* what works.
- *Balance between what is paid to various levels for their work (internal equity)*
  - ○ In so many of the surveys we have conducted, internal equity of pay was much more important than external competitiveness. The latter had to be competitive to get a person into the job, so it was a "given;" the former was the challenge. Since so much informal internal communication (including "gossip") centers on pay, big differences made big news. Organizations have found that they had better have rational and easily explained methodologies for how they set pay internally, and they had better communicate those to their workers. *This is especially true for pay differences between men and women, for similar or the same jobs.* In most advanced countries these are illegal, but whether they are or not, *they can demoralize large sections of our workforce.* Far better to focus on a job's "size" in determining its pay, which is a *gender-neutral and incumbent neutral* methodology of job evaluation very familiar to those who work in compensation. Too often in the past, pay has been set only by market surveys which tended to perpetuate the inequalities that we have seen in how "women's jobs" are paid versus "men's jobs." An *engagement-friendly* practice to redress this *unfair imbalance* and then communicate it widely is a good step forward. We can—and should—easily *track* all pay issues like this in a good workforce opinion survey.
  - ○ CEO versus average worker pay is also in this category; here, some organizations have decided that taking very good care of one person *unbalances* things for everyone else, as we saw in Chapter 3.
- *Balance between stock purchase plans, stock options and employee ownership at different organizational levels*
  - ○ We cannot ignore the aspect of *stock options/stock plans* and their cousin *employee ownership.* Why should options be the territory only of

leadership? Why not make the workers also owners, even if only of a small part? Bring some *balance* into this equation, turn "employees" into those owners and see what happens to their engagement and performance. Anyone who has started their own business, as we both have more than once, knows that there is a world of difference in internal emotional state and behavior when one owns. Getting up in the middle of the night to take care of a client's needs somewhere across the world? No problem! Fortunately, the European Federation of Employee Share Ownership shows that since the Crash there is an increase in the number of organizations participating in its namesake practice. The 2010 Economic Survey they carried out[60] said:

> The number of employee owners was nearly 10 million in 2010 in large European companies (out of 32.6 million employees). The number of companies that have employee ownership was increasing (91.7%), as well as those having share plans for all employees (53.7%) and those with stock option plans (64.1%). However, significant differences can be seen between countries: A significant increase in the number of employee owners in Spain, Poland, France and the Nordic countries (Denmark, Sweden, Norway, Finland), contrasting with a significant decrease in Belgium, Ireland and The Netherlands.

In the United States, stock option grants seem to be falling in number, partly as a result of some scandals related to accounting shenanigans called "backdating," or gaming the system in order to increase payouts. The Crash also did not help stock options' reputation, by making most of them worthless.[61]

In spite of this US-specific trend, some form of ownership is a good idea. This is because one thing most organizations try to do to increase the probability of worker engagement is to *make them feel like owners.* What better way to do this than to *actually make them owners*? The 2009 UK MacLeod Report on employee engagement emphasized this with a comment on the benefits of worker ownership, itself provided by the (UK) *Employee Ownership Association,* referring to their study as *"Good Business – the employee ownership experience":*

> 96 companies' own views of the experience of employee ownership [were surveyed]. Ninety-one per cent said greater employee commitment was "the biggest win of being employee owned"; 81 per cent said staff take on more responsibility; 72 per cent said staff worked harder; 66 per cent believed staff were more innovative; and 61 per cent said they were more productive.[62]

- *Balance between base and incentive pay*
  - ○ Here we revisit the issue of competition versus cooperation, and team-work versus individual focus. They both come into play when it comes to rewards. Organizations know that pay policies are not some arcane aspect of HR but are *central to the culture they create*. Change an incentive plan, move it from individual to team, and the reaction is immediate and not always favorable. Money talks, and often with a loud voice! Again, *balance and alignment with cultural values* is key. Knowing what your workforce thinks about these issues is crucial to decision making here.
- *Balance between hiring from outside and "growing your own"*
  - ○ In the vast business that is talent acquisition and development, a key issue is whether this talent is produced inside the organization or not. The *engagement-friendly* approach would seem to favor "home grown" for the incentives and rewards that it provides to "insiders" versus the talent pool hungry[63] to get a chance at working at that organization. There is some evidence that "talent acquisition" is shifting to a mindset that is closely related to worker engagement and away from one in which talent has to be grabbed from outside as fast and frequently as possible.[64] Since one of the best methods for creating a high engagement work environment is to *allow and encourage people to be their very best*, this can uncover hidden talent in people already in the organization, rather than require an automatic search outside. In turn this can have nothing but an enhancing effect on engagement levels.
- *Sustainability: Physical health and wellness*
  - ○ When we planned our first book together, on morale, engagement and performance,[65] we did not have the idea to include health and wellness as performance factors. We were going to concentrate instead on productivity, profitability and customer satisfaction. Then we discovered that there was a veritable treasure trove of research on the connection between how people feel at work and their *physical health*, and decided to cover it in depth. This is a major issue of *sustainability*: workers who are healthy will be able to stay longer with the organization, by definition have less time off for sickness, be happier and much more productive. They will also cost far less, as far as any health plan is concerned. This is why health is such a big performance *and sustainability* factor, at least partly driven by engagement at work. The boss from hell is clearly a dangerous animal, as some astounding research demonstrates.[66] A "healthy organization" may be defined in many ways, but it begins by being one in which its workers' physical health is sustained by creating an *engagement-friendly environment* to which they can come (or connect) every day.
- *Sustainability: Psychological health, happiness at work and other factors*
  - ○ Sustainability means more than a physically healthy workplace, as much as that is a great thing to have. This is because the term "healthy

organization" applies to more than physical health, but also to *psychological health and well-being*. What contributes to this? By definition, the high engagement work environment is one that raises psychological well-being among its workforce. As we have seen, that is the first step in the process of engagement. A psychologically hurtful environment will not only erode any engagement levels that were there (with all the many performance-draining effects which come about as a result of that), it will have other effects. A workplace that burns people out through various misguided aspects of its culture *is not a sustainable one.* Yes, it can function for a period of time, it can cycle through a lot of workers who leave as soon as they can, but over time it will not sustain itself. Far better to create an environment where people feel good and, yes, where they are *happy*.

○ This is something that has more and more focus in the organizational world: *happiness of workers.* Now there are a lot of managers who would never want to make that a goal, seeing it as antagonistic to the hard-nosed mission of their organization. But they would be wrong. There is now plenty of evidence that happiness at work can indeed be a worthwhile goal because it is highly engaging to be happy and vice versa. Listen to what a Gallup study had to say about how happiness and engagement go hand in hand:

> A clear majority of engaged workers—86%—said they very often felt happy while at work. Among low-engagement respondents, only 11% of actively disengaged and 48% of not-engaged employees stated that they, too, were very often happy at work … Happy employees are better equipped to handle workplace relationships, stress, and change.[67]

Some might question the directionality of this relationship and say that this is a chicken and egg situation. For us, it is clear that this is *a loop*: happiness (with the environment in which one finds oneself) precedes worker engagement, and engagement in turn makes people happy. This relationship is very compelling: the idea of going to work every day and expecting to be happy instead of dreading the experience—can we only imagine the benefits that accrue from this? We don't have to guess, we dedicated a whole book to the performance outcomes of engagement and morale. Interestingly, several groups are dedicated to studying the science of happiness at work, and there are increasing amounts of research that solidify the happiness-engagement-productivity connection.[68,69] One of us recently co-authored a book on the subject of happiness and well-being at work, with an emphasis on its productivity connections.[70]

We have one caveat here though: be careful of those who would tell you that one can be highly engaged at work but miserable and with one foot out of the door,[71] that engagement is some kind of coercive, "top-down" thing that is "done to" people who don't want it, that only happiness (and not engagement) is related to performance,[72] and that "happiness at work" has now replaced engagement as the newest "must have" thing at work. This is all nonsense! Engaged people make that choice out of free will, just as a horse chooses to drink water. Secondly, highly engaged people do so out of a sense of well-being we call "high morale," a positive emotional state. Being miserable in a job and being highly engaged is therefore impossible, in our view: being productive and miserable, yes, but not truly engaged. Just look at a sweatshop and you see productive, often miserable, but certainly not engaged workers. A truly engaged individual does not have one foot out the door and one eye on the Internet job sites! It is also true that while engaged people are usually happy, not all happy people may be engaged: *happiness (i.e. a sense of well-being) is necessary but not sufficient for engagement. An individual can be quite happy and content but not especially productive.* That person is not *engaged*. Similarly, a person can be quite happy at work, until she meets *the boss from hell*. We will then see how long that "happiness" lasts. One way that the happiness-at-work specialists get around these issues is by redefining happiness at work as something quite different to normal "happiness in life".[73] When we read what they have to say though, they have essentially taken morale, engagement and even job satisfaction and defined them all as "happiness at work." Of course, these things happen all the time, and we have even complained at times that engagement practitioners took the decades-old and very useful concept of morale, repackaged it and served it up as fresh and new![74] As far as *only happiness* being related to and driving performance (such as productivity, customer satisfaction, etc.), we wrote a whole book on how morale and engagement relate to and *drive these things*[75] and are not about to concede that happiness (even as carefully redefined) has usurped this role!

Having said all this there is something very positive about what the happiness-at-work people do, which some employee engagement specialists have neglected: they train people to feel good at work, in other words *they help people to engage*. As we have seen, there are two parts to engagement, the environment at work, or culture, which we are focusing on in depth, and the individual choice to engage. By enhancing the skills necessary to make and carry out this choice, they are adding great value. However, in doing so, they do not need to throw the whole "engagement" baby out with the bath water, by pretending that they have totally replaced engagement with a redefined concept of "happiness"!

Leaf through any good book on engagement, morale or best management practices and you will find many examples of how the aforesaid processes are used in the most successful companies. As an example, each year *Fortune* magazine of the US selects the *100 Best Companies To Work For*;[76] in 2011, *Fortune* highlighted three US companies that were highly ranked in this beauty contest, and it is interesting to see how their best practices line up with what we have discussed earlier:

- The wildly successful online apparel and footwear company *Zappos* has HR staff veto new hires who they think will not be a good cultural "fit."
- *Zappos* will also *not allow senior employees to receive benefits that are not given to junior workers.*
- Hollywood filmmaker *Dreamworks Animation* gives its workers free dry cleaning, meals and medical care on campus so that they can focus on work.
- *If they need to make changes to save money, Dreamworks* also cuts "anything but people," including in the period after the Crash.
- *Teach for America*, a nonprofit that supplies young teachers to schools in poorer localities, allows its staff to work from home, as long as they get the work done.

### Applying *BEST practices* to all that you do. 3: People

Your people are both affected by the processes we have examined before, and some—but not all—serve to carry those processes forward and bring the culture to "life." Whether manager or individual contributor, do your people act to embody and enhance the culture you wish to have; are they a neutral force in that regard; or are they actually a negative, destructive force, pushing against it at every stage? In any organization of a certain size there will be all three of these at work. Your job is to maximize those in category 1: the enhancers, those who carry the torch forward at their own level, and make the culture "real." Perhaps you made a major effort to hire such people, knowing in great detail exactly what values and behaviors would fit your culture? Perhaps you already had people who were not hired with such rigor, but who were open enough to be inspired by the culture you have and willing to buy into it wholeheartedly? Whatever the case, one cannot ignore the fact that without your people, the culture never comes to life.

This brings us to the issue of personality, and as we have discussed elsewhere in this book, not everyone will buy in to the vision you have for the culture of your organization, no matter how great that is and how well you treat them. The trick is to avoid such people in the first place, or (as a less attractive alternative) to let them go if you have the misfortune to have brought them on board and already allowed them to do some damage. Well-worn metaphors, like one apple spoiling the whole barrel, have become well worn for a reason: they have great truths in them!

Applying *BEST practices* to your hiring and promotions is one good way to ensure that your people fit the culture you wish to have in your organization. Is your new hire able to *balance* things like competitiveness and cooperation in ways that fit your organization's values and needs? Or did you hire—or promote—a competitive "lone ranger" for a team-oriented job? Just knowing that one answer can save you countless problems with that individual, and that team, in the future. Is the individual you just placed in that management job really the most *engagement-friendly* or simply the best accountant, engineer, salesperson from the team? Will the new hire enable you to *sustain* your culture, which requires that every individual do their part to carry it forward, along with tens, hundreds or perhaps thousands of other people working together toward that goal? Of course, the final element of the ***BEST** test, tracking*, is also crucial in knowing, for example, how your hiring and promotion decisions are affecting your culture and engagement levels. Do you *track* the effect of managers on your workforce, and how they affect morale and engagement? If not, you simply have no idea what is happening "out there," whether the culture and values you say are so important to you are really being lived "in the trenches."

*Remember that managers have more impact on worker engagement levels than anything else in the organization.* We cannot therefore finish this chapter without looking in more depth at the critical importance of this.

### *Tracking: Knowing where you are and from where you have come*

Tracking means that you have data on where you are, how far you need to go, and in which direction! Tracking is GPS for your organization's culture. Now we recognize that there is somewhat of a backlash against surveys, which are our methodology of choice for accomplishing this job. We see this backlash in blogs with titles that don't hold back, like *"You Don't Need No Stinkin' Surveys to Measure Engagement"*![77] Actually, sorry to say this, but you do—unless perhaps you have only 77 co-workers like the author of that blog, and the CEO can have them all in his back garden for pizza every Friday night. Even then, a survey might, indeed probably would, be needed. There is simply no other way to collect this kind of information from your workforce; we have blogged about this, because it is so important.[78] Forget about bumping into people and asking them about how things are going, then generalizing this to the whole: you have just committed some major scientific errors and your data is not valid! Trust us when we say that companies like Google have the right idea by surveying on a regular basis (in Google's case, a large 100-item survey called *Google Geist* every year and smaller surveys every few months).[79] Google is in fact a jobs program for Ph.D.s in our field because the company places so much emphasis on their surveys, and like true engineers they analyze it in great depth. You may not need to go that far, although we believe Google gains enormous benefit from their emphasis in this area; but at least follow their example in knowing where you stand.

One issue that comes up is whether you should be using a short questionnaire such as Gallup's proprietary *Q-12* or something longer and more comprehensive. We vote for longer: a longer survey does not have to be so time consuming[80] and gives you a huge advantage. That is the opportunity to find out not just *whether your people are engaged but why* (or if not, why not). "Why" will in turn tell you where and which best practices are being used in your organization, so that others may learn from and use them. We strongly recommend you take that route: not only will a longer survey answer the "why" question, it will allow you to examine aspects of your culture with custom questions, in ways that short surveys cannot even begin to do. In summary, *don't do your culture work in the dark*: surveys will shine the light you need, deep into your organization, so you can move forward.

We have taken a journey here through several aspects of organizational life and the many decisions we have to make, and looked at this through the ***BEST** practices* lens. This is not meant to be comprehensive, but is designed instead to give you a template with which to work in your own organization. Can you meet the needs for *balance, engagement-friendliness and sustainability*? Can you *track* where you have started from and how much progress you have made? If so, you have created something that will move you toward a work culture that will bring many rewards.

## Conclusions

This chapter has been dedicated to the culture in your organization, defining its requirements and suggesting that it can be crafted in a way that will *greatly enhance the engagement of your workers*. We have proposed that a successful high engagement culture should be built on universal principles, specifically *balance*, and in particular balance between *"me" and "we"* and between *competition and cooperation*. We have been careful not to "throw the baby out with the bathwater," meaning that we fully accept that lurching from one "side" to another as a reaction to the Crash is a huge mistake. Balance gives us a chance to see the *good that comes from both competition and cooperation*, for example.

Our requirements for the high engagement culture were summarized in the ***BEST*** acronym detailed in this chapter and we promised that they would not be "pie in the sky." These ideas work. We know this because we have studied in depth two organizations that live and breathe the ***BEST** practices* every day. They demonstrate that these ideas are not just dreams, but a reality that provides some with huge advantage. We will take a look at these organizations now.

# 5
# Case Studies for the High Engagement Culture: BMW Group and Whole Foods Market

## Introduction

We selected two outstanding companies to feature in our case studies for the high engagement culture. Two companies that are on either side of the Atlantic from each other, in very different businesses. One in manufacturing and one in food retailing. One in Germany and the other in the United States. Yet they are joined by the fact that they treat their workers with a respect and fairness that is a beacon for those who doubt that what we have talked about up to this point is more than idealistic, or for those who think that these are great ideas but are impractical and hard to actualize. These companies do this year after year and their performance underscores that this is no touchy-feely exercise. Indeed they are both world class and leaders in their industry, and as we write, are enjoying record stock prices and/or financial results.

## BMW Group, Munich, Germany

BMW Group's world headquarters sits, very appropriately, near a busy street packed with many of its products moving around the city of Munich at a very restrained (for "Bimmers" (cars) or "Beemers" (motorcycles)) 50km/hour, or much slower in rush hours. If you want to move between southern and northern parts of the inner city, you will probably find yourself on the *Mittler Ring*, and you will see the four towers rising up before you, like four giant engine cylinders, with the familiar black and "Bavarian blue and white" logo on top. The design, appropriately known as the *Vierzylinder*, is a well-known German landmark and source of pride for the city of Munich. On the large campus, in addition to the *Vierzylinder*, is a manufacturing facility; *BMW Welt* where people (often from overseas) go to pick up their new cars and look at the latest offerings; and the marvelous BMW Museum. The latter is built like the famous Guggenheim museum in New York, with a round dome containing a circular walking route down through the history of BMW with its automobiles, motor-cycles and an aircraft engine hanging at the beginning of the walk. Bimmer/Beemer fans must consider this a place of pilgrimage, and one of us saw plenty of them on a visit. Here, the past meets the future as old BMW autos bring back memories and look quaint compared to the beasts available today, ready for the captains of German industry who wish to be whisked (or whisk themselves) around at great speed by 12-cylinder engines tuned for the *Autobahn*.[1] This is balanced (we like that word) with the new hybrid models and a hydrogen car that emits only water vapor as its end product, ready for a world that is not yet here, one in which hydrogen can be produced without, itself, needing enor-mous amounts of energy to be extracted.

The company has been in operation since 1917[2] and, as we write, has just come off a record year. Things were not always so rosy: in 1959 the company was in serious financial difficulties and had to consider, and rejected, bank-ruptcy. The rescue came in the form of an outside investment that remains in place to this day:

> The controlling majority shareholder of the BMW Aktiengesellschaft since 1959 is the Quandt family, which owns about 46% of the stock. The rest is in public float.[3]

Hit quite hard by the 2008 Crash and subsequent deep recession, BMW has bounced back quickly thanks to soaring demand for its products from emerg-ing middle and upper-middle class consumers in Asia, especially China. Indeed the company has established a factory there, at the Tiexi and Dadong sites in Shenyang.

BMW Group builds the namesake brand of automobiles and motorcycles, Rolls Royce Motor Cars and MINI of the UK, and Husqvarna motorcycles. Sales in 2010 reached €60.5 billion and profits of €4.836 billion. The snapback from recession levels has been extraordinary; consider that profits in 2008 were €330 million and slipped even further to €210 million in 2009. This reflects the per-formance Germany has experienced in its powerhouse export industries across many sectors and that has driven unemployment down far faster than in other European countries and in the US. The company was recently ranked 79 out of the 500 largest companies in the world (for 2010), in a list compiled by the US *Fortune* magazine.[4]

### Why we picked BMW as a case study

Not long ago one of us was writing a blog about US executive compensation, going over some of the data that we have shared with you in this book, and complaining that this was an unsustainable and unfair situation, which none-theless had sustained itself for a long time. We asked ourselves, as we do in this book: *isn't there a better way of doing things?* A search, as usual on Google, brought up an extraordinary quote from BMW. Here is what we said in 2010[5]:

> Munich-based BMW last year also became the first big company in Germany to implement bonuses based on reasonable ratios compared to the average worker's bonus. The company spokesman was quoted as saying *"We don't just want to build sustainable cars. We also want to have sustainable personnel politics. We think this is good for the company culture"*.[6] Ahh how refreshing that he places personal, selfish interests lower than that of a sustainable culture for his workforce. Is this one of the reasons why BMW has, and continues to make, such great cars?

It was clear at this point that BMW should be featured in this book since its philosophy is closely aligned to what we are putting forward:

- A balance between "me" (on the part of top management) with "we" (the workforce) designed specifically to enhance the relationship between the two "levels."
- A clear statement that this is the intention, sending a message out to the workforce that this is a core part of company culture.

BMW does this because it believes, as we do, that its workforce is their most important asset. Here is how they put it in a special publication available online that sets out their "sustainability" goals with regard to employees:

> "Employees are our number one success factor. This is why human resources decisions are among the key decisions we take." This statement is one of the basic principles stipulated in BMW Group's corporate Strategy Number ONE which are the foundation for the present advancement of the company's human resources and social policies and thus of the entire field of personnel work.[7]

Let's be clear here: Strategy Number ONE drives BMW forward in all aspects of its operations. The statement about people is at the core of this. In light of what else they could have picked—such as their engineering prowess, their brand image, their manufacturing skills, their high levels of innovation—it is interesting that people are their choice for the "top spot." Of course, it is people who are the engineers, the innovators, the manufacturers. BMW understands where it all starts, where it succeeds or fails, and they have no wish to hurt this "number one success factor" by their behavior at the top.

Like all the best companies in the world, BMW's culture is underpinned by core values (called "principles") translated into expected behaviors. Bearing in mind our ***BEST*** *practices* covered in the last chapter, it is useful to look at these, from the 2010 BMW Annual Report[8]:

*Customer focus*
The success of our company is determined by our customers. They are at the heart of everything we do. The results of all our activities must be valued in terms of the benefits they will generate for our customers.

*Peak performance*
We aim to be the best—a challenge to which all of us must rise. Each and every employee must be prepared to deliver peak performance. We strive to be among the elite, but without being arrogant. *It is the company and its products that count—and nothing else.*

*Responsibility*
Every BMW Group employee takes personal responsibility for the company's success. When working in a team, each employee must assume personal responsibility for his or her actions. In doing so we are fully aware that we are working towards achieving the company's goals. For this reason, we work together in the best interests of the company.

*Effectiveness*
The only results that count for the company are those which have a *sustainable impact*. In assessing leadership, we must consider the effectiveness of performance on results.

*Adaptability*
In order to ensure our long-term success we must adapt to new challenges with speed and flexibility. We therefore see change as an opportunity—adaptability as essential to be able to capitalise on it.

*Frankness*
As we strive to find the best solution, *it is each employee's duty to express any opposing opinions they may have.* The solutions we agree upon will then be consistently implemented by all those involved.

*Respect, trust, fairness*
We treat each other with respect. Leadership is based on mutual trust. *Trust is rooted in fairness* and reliability.

*Employees*
People make companies. *Our employees are the strongest factor in our success, which means our personnel decisions will be among the most important we ever make.*

*Leading by example*
Every manager must lead by example.

*Sustainability*
In our view, *sustainability constitutes a lasting contribution to the success of the company*. This is the basis upon which we assume ecological and social responsibility.

*Society*
Social responsibility is an integral part of our corporate self-image.

*Independence*
We secure the corporate independence of the BMW Group through sustained profitable growth.

(emphasis added)

This is a remarkable list; *it is BMW at its core*. The challenge is then to live these "principles." Also interesting is the overlap between our **BEST** *practices* and this list. Does the list pass the **BEST** *test*? We believe that with its emphasis on sustainability (a prism through which all employee actions are seen), a stated goal of "fairness" (itself a sustainability factor, as well as an engagement-friendly one), and the clear statement that "arrogance" will not be tolerated, it goes a long way toward meeting our goals. Social responsibility is also highly valued by most workers we have seen surveyed, raising engagement levels. As an example of how the BMW principles fit with our ideal of a toned-down ego at work, think back to Chapter 3 on that subject and overlay that with the previous statement that:

It is the company and its products that count—and nothing else.

How the ego would hate that! NO room for "me"? Unacceptable!

When one looks at the compensation section of the 2010 annual report, it is clear that BMW practices what they preach. Interestingly, even the top management team (called the "management board") is on a set of fixed base salaries, the likes of which one would almost never see in the US. Incoming individuals received (in 2010) a base of €420,000, and after two years this bumps up to €480,000. Of course, this is enhanced by variable and incentive compensation, and a typical member of this seven-person team that runs the company worldwide received over €2,000,000 in total compensation in 2010. This is a lot of money to most people but peanuts for a company that was just rated (in the US *Fortune* magazine) at the 79th place in the annual roundup of the world's largest companies. Remember that Jack Welch's retirement package alone, before he gave most of it back, was $8,000,000 a year! The total compensation of *all seven of BMW's top managers in fiscal year 2010* was only €18,172,350,[9] an amount at which many US executives would scoff if offered that much for themselves alone! If we assume that the average worker at BMW makes about €75,000 in combined salary, bonus and benefits, the ratio of top management to worker compensation is a little over 25:1, a far cry from some of the numbers we have examined elsewhere, but not unusual for Germany. If the €75,000 sounds high, it is because BMW makes it a point to pay in the top one third of all companies in a given region, and in Germany manufacturing worker pay and benefits are among the highest in the world. BMW also pays temporary workers, of which it has an increasing number to ensure flexibility, at the same rate as "tariff" (mutually negotiated—with the union—rates). As far as we know, this is quite unprecedented: a feature of temporary workers is usually not only that they can be quickly let go if conditions require that, but also that they are "cheaper." BMW wants none of that "cheapness" and prides itself, as we shall see in our interview, that these workers are not treated as "second class citizens." It is another sign of their culture in action.

One way an organization demonstrates that it is balancing the drives of the individual ego with the needs of the organization as a whole is by making compensation dependent on performance. Then when someone is well paid, it is because they performed, not because they were "entitled" simply as a member of top management. BMW makes their top team's compensation very dependent on performance, driving the leveraged portion (in other words the part of compensation that is "at risk" if performance drops) to 80% as against the base of 20%, when targets are met.[10] In our experience, pay for performance plans *that are well designed* increase a sense among workers that the culture is driven by a degree of fairness, a word that we have stressed in these pages is central to high engagement levels. By placing so much of top management compensation at risk, the level of perceived fairness across the organization has a chance to be higher.

Of course, Germany being a highly unionized work environment due to a quite heavy hand of regulation (by most standards outside of Europe, but normal for much of Europe), this type of compensation leverage is much less for the average worker. That person is paid according to the "tariff," with little chance to reward individual initiative. If this seems balanced in the wrong direction, we would tend to agree, but German society seems to want to continue with the way things are; and as we shall see, BMW's workers do not seem like an unhappy bunch, based on the limited survey data to which we had access. A job with BMW is highly coveted, and applications for apprenticeships there run high. Students in the Universum annual survey of undergraduates and university graduates in Europe rated the company as one of the top three companies to work for in both 2008 and 2009, the top company in Germany and the top automobile company in the world.[11] The 2011 survey for Europe shows that engineers still want to work at BMW (fourth place) much more than at Daimler/Mercedes-Benz (26th place for male engineers, 65th for women), although Audi has leapt forward from 2010 into the second spot, giving BMW a run for its money.[12]

### Interview with Harald Krüger, Member of the Board of Management, BMW Group

Our curiosity about BMW and its culture, kindled by the quote about executive compensation, was only partly satisfied by already-published material (annual reports and other documents that detail people-oriented strategies and values, for example). We needed to go much deeper and the only way was by inter-viewing someone at the top of the organization. One of us (DB) was fortunate to be able to meet for almost an hour with Harald Krüger, a Member of the seven-person Board of Management, which is headed by the CEO and runs the company worldwide. Herr Krüger is an interesting person, with an engineering background and at the time of our interview (summer 2011) was only 45 years old, the youngest member of the Board. Most of his career has been spent in BMW, with stints at the US plant in Spartanburg, South Carolina; in England at the Hams Hall engine factory; and in Munich. His job at the time of the interview was to head global personnel and industrial relations, which was the reason for our desire to talk to him: Harald Krüger is the person at BMW with a day-to-day responsibility to think about and talk about the company's culture, among many other things. He ensures that human resource decisions, seen within BMW as *"among the key decisions we take,"* reflect those values. No doubt, all BMW managers are also mindful of this and find it their responsibility to live the values we have detailed previously.

The interview kicked off with a background discussion about this book and its goals and focus, and as part of this we talked about the case study in our 2009 book, and the findings concerning the strong connections we found there between morale/engagement and customer satisfaction. Herr Krüger started by pointing out that BMW asks questions in its regular employee surveys directly on "customer orientation" and compares that to external benchmarks of other companies' responses. The interview then continued:

*DAVID BOWLES: Well we certainly want to get to that and I look forward to discussing it with you. Now the new book is different and what it does is start with the Crash and asks the question "is there a better way of doing things;" in particular, we want to look at raising engagement levels by finding a balance between "me" and "we."*

HARALD KRÜGER: That is a great topic David, and it is something which interested me when you made the interview request. You see, I took on the new role exactly at the beginning of the crisis. I started on December 1 [2008] and I was in a position to see both perspectives. I can honestly say that achieving our targets in 2011 was only possible because we handled things right in the crisis—from the management perspective, as far as respect goes, and regarding corporate culture. Because our people saw that we treated them with respect in the crisis; they were willing to return the show of commitment in the recovery, which was much more than what we expected. I've seen differences in how other companies and leaders and managers were operating in the crisis; and you can see what happened with companies that didn't respond in an appropriate manner. They had real issues in the ramp-up phase.

*DB: That is so interesting. I think that when companies treat their employees well it is like a vaccine, so that when a "virus" like this Crash comes along, the company is "inoculated" so to speak. It means you can survive the bad times better. But let's talk about a specific aspect of management on which the book focuses, the ego. It seems to us that when that first-line manager is ego-driven, the team members have to spend half their time managing the boss' ego.*

HK: This can be the case and we look into this very much. It is why we want our managers to have their *"feet on the ground."* For example, we have started a new initiative for the future management generations, including our top management, which is incorporated into our management and leadership training. BMW Group graduates were recognized last year for their efforts in corporate social volunteering. We have now incorporated this initiative into every single program for young people coming into the BMW Group, as well as for management levels, so that they remain with their feet on the ground, that they respect individuals, that they treat everyone fairly. We also incorporated this into the management training as a basic principle and everyone is required to do it. The feedback is enormously positive from the new management graduates. For example, they were playing soccer with kids in a neighborhood of Munich that has issues with poverty and crime, and were incorporating these principles there. Now we have activities like this in the apprenticeship programs and in programs for future top management.

*DB: There is a lot of controversy in our field as to whether engagement has been affected by the Crash, and if so to what extent. Some consultants like Gallup say that engagement is flat in the states even with everything we have been through.*

HK: I'm not sure I believe that—perhaps there are some signs, but just on the surface. Take one of our plants here in Dingolfing and the assembly line employees there, for example. It's about 100 km north of here [Munich].

During the economic downturn, these people had their number of working days reduced by nine or ten days a month. This had never happened to them before—it came about due to circumstances beyond our control. These employees were affected by something which had nothing to do with them. They began to feel "I don't have a safe job and my work time has been reduced." This is something they will never forget, that feeling of not being safe and not knowing how long this is going to last. This is the feeling I came away with after speaking with many of them.

What we did during that time was to stand close to our employees and we said to them "yes, because of the short-time work we will be paying you less." In actual fact, we paid them more than we were legally obliged to. We paid them 93% net compared with the legal minimum of 60% under German law. I believed strongly at that time that things would change for the better one day. And therefore, if we demonstrated to them that we stood by them when times were hard and that we made sure that they had money at their disposal, I believed that when things got better they would pay back the respect we had shown. So when things did get better and we needed additional shifts on Saturdays, they [the employees] came back to us and said, "yes, we will give you the time because you committed to us before, and we will work those extra shifts now." It paid off enormously; the 93% was a commitment and a statement that "the company stands behind you." It gave us great opportunities and flexibility and the ability to do huge volumes, so the payoff was very significant. And this experience, they never ever had that in the last 50 years in that region; that something which happened with Lehman Brothers [in New York] could affect their jobs.

*DB: Let's talk about executive pay. One of the reasons we wanted you as a case study in the book is because of an article we saw in Der Spiegel online. You are quoted in this article and we have repeated another quote in the book, that executive pay is controlled in order to essentially enhance the relationship with your workforce, what you call "sustainable personnel politics." Can you tell us where this decision came from and whether you target a specific ratio between executives and the rest of your workforce or you use some other method?*

*Herr Krüger began his reply by explaining that the company does not target a specific top management to average worker ratio in its compensation practices. He then set out the company philosophy and practices with regard to pay:*

HK: Let me explain how we determine pay for almost everyone in the company. First of all, we want to be in the top third in the region in which we are operating, whether it is the worker on the assembly line or management. For management pay we have three main portions, first of all the base salary, which as you would expect is determined by local conditions of competitiveness, skills and so on, both for the line employees and managers. Then we have two bonuses, one personal performance-based and one company-based. What is unique to the industry is that we use one formula for the company bonus throughout BMW AG [the German part of BMW, as opposed to its foreign subsidiaries]. Obviously with different payouts, but that formula is the same right across the company—from senior jobs to the line employees and everyone knows this formula. The formula incorporates the financial success of the company, as well as being linked to the dividend. This links everyone to the company's success and is one of our core HR policies. It's open, fair and transparent. In many countries, except Germany, where this instrument is legally not available, managers will rate their associates, which results in the personal bonus. This way we can acknowledge, promote and reward good individual performance within the team. BMW follows three philosophies: (1) to treat people fairly (2) to be competitive on every level and to always be an attractive employer, (3) transparency: we apply the same principles no matter if it is senior top management or any other level.

*Herr Krüger then went into some technical details as to how BMW controls the pay gap between different levels of employees in the company. They achieve this by having the uniform payout percentage for company performance across all of BMW that we have seen earlier, while basing this payout on what he called "corridors" or bands of base amounts on which this percentage is calculated. Those bands are rigorously controlled for internal equity, while at the same time being flexible enough to maintain external competitiveness. He then went on to explain that BMW has more flexible pay than others in their industry:*

HK: At the management level, BMW does have much more variable pay than its competitors. In the middle-manager ranks base pay is about 70% and variable pay 30%, whereas with our competition you normally find variable pay at this level is about 15–20%.[13]

*DB: Let's switch a little bit and talk about the values at BMW that drive you and drive your culture here. You've been here quite a while, since 1992 in fact, so you have been able to observe this. Do the values come from BMW's history, its current management team, the ownership family? Or is it a combination of this? Obviously the choices you make in the area of personnel are all driven by this, these values.*

HK: To answer your question, it's a combination. Let me explain: back in 2007, the board and the management team defined Strategy Number ONE in 2007, which consists of 12 "basic principles." [We have listed these before.] This was interesting because we didn't just work on strategies for the business, we also decided to work on a set of core corporate values, which everyone should be measured against and which everyone should actively promote and live within the company. Secondly, it [our culture] is also driven by our history and our ownership, but especially by the experience of almost losing our autonomy back in 1959 and 1960. We had to fight for our individuality and independence. This drives the company now as well. This experience also had a strong influence on the relationship between management and the works council members. At that time BMW also resolved a lot of issues within the company before going public. The works council and the management team worked closely together to resolve these issues. This goes back to 1959 and 1960, and by standing side by side we learned to work together and helped to secure the future of the company. Both sides have the same interest: the future development and growth of the company. Also pertaining to its history, BMW is driven strongly by product orientation. This is very much part of BMW's genes, not just engineering but also very much strong brand management. If you look at MINI, if you look at Rolls-Royce, managing premium brands is one of our major strengths. If you look at today's culture therefore there is definitely input from all of these areas.

*DB: Now you survey your employees on a regular basis so you know if the culture is being lived or just being talked about by top management. What do your surveys tell you, if you don't mind sharing it with me, about what your strengths are in terms of the culture, and what do they tell you about what needs to be improved? I notice that some survey came back and said something about "top management style" or "leadership style." Can you share something about this?*

HK: What has been consistent is that we are doing this survey in a cycle of every two or three years; for example, our last survey was completed by 78,000 people across the Group and we do it at the same time across the world. In the past we would start in Germany and so on, and now we do it in three weeks worldwide. It's absolutely confidential and voluntary, and that's why we have 95,000 associates around the world with 78,000 responding. So we are quite satisfied with the rate of involvement and it shows that all the statistics are absolutely valid. What does it demonstrate? First of all, that there is a very strong identification by the associates with the company, with the BMW Group, at all levels. For example, there is one question "do you like to work at BMW?" and the results are always very good, *even during the crisis*. We also see people who are very satisfied with the salaries, fringe benefits and so on.

Also the people are very product driven and not just the managers, or the R&D department, and we find this across the world. So when you look at the 12 basic principles with the survey results you can see that, yes, we also have areas of improvement.

We can see that in a crisis, areas like employers' and employees' engagement levels need to increase. We also saw in the crisis that there was more insecurity; we also see the need for more trust, more speed, deciding quicker, things like that. These are areas where we would like to be even better. Compared with the competition, we are above average—in some areas we are well above average—but it is essentially about keeping people motivated, to keep striving and setting even higher standards, to be number one in all areas. For me as a board member, this is exactly the position to be in otherwise it would be boring! There is another finding from the survey results and that is that they are locally and regionally different. Why is that?

*DB: I was going to ask you about that, is there an overriding sense of cultural values that you have around the world and how do you balance that with local values and strengths?*

HK: We need things that are paramount around the world but yes I am a friend of both aspects. We need all the local strengths! For example, I lived in the UK for three and half years in Oxford: I loved living there because people were so open to change. If you just explain why we need to change they have very little resistance. In the UK, I felt that if you give people the feeling that you have your whole heart in the matter and you are thinking in the right direction, with a clear vision, I felt I always had the trust of people there. I am a great believer in using the local strengths—you have to strive to get the best out of people and strengthen the strengths in the various cultures. On the other hand, yes, we do need to have some things which are consistent around the world. For example, respect and fairness; this is part of our corporate set of values and something which is defined by us. That's why I believe in the local strengths, in the local opportunities that those present, but also being consistent across the world especially in those two areas. I would add that we strive for worldwide consistency in engineering, as well as being process and quality driven—to deliver premium products, to deliver premium services, to keep the customer fascinated—that cannot be at one level in one country, on another level in another country. That is absolutely where we control things in terms of the quality of the culture.

*DB: With your culture and these values do you enforce it when somebody violates these values in some way? Are you very strict with this and do you come down very hard in these situations? Or you just say, "well it's okay, you're having a bad day" and so?*

HK: We do three things: first of all, the managers are driving the culture and they need to lead by example. Secondly, in our performance review we split the business results from the personal performance so we look at two things like what targets you've achieved in terms of business and then *how* they are achieved. Is the team led by example? Is the team motivated? So we look independently and equally at the personal side of the manager. How does he or she [the manager] explain our business strategy? Are they motivating people, are they promoting people and are they developing people? Are they only going with the best people on their teams and never taking the risk of developing others? So we are assessing this equally and the final performance review is a combination of both business results and team management. By looking at both things we have made a big jump in ensuring that the culture is right. Third, we use a 360° review process[14] for managers. We also use the associates' survey results. For example, each of my direct reports had to present the results for their area, including the strengths and the weaknesses. So this is how we do the checks and balances.

*DB: Now let's look at the years from 2007 to 2011; you have about 12,000 fewer employees during that time period. You talked about the impact, going through the recession, on your factory 100 km north of here in Dingolfing, and we've also talked about how treating employees well has inoculated BMW to some extent from the effects of this Crash. But I was chatting with some people here in Germany about how they see BMW and it was interesting how they responded: they said, "oh they have all these temporary employees." And I know that on TV last night, while there was a lot of good news about BMW, they focused almost completely on this temporary worker situation. Perhaps you can comment about these temporary employees for us?*

HK: During the recession, I want to make it clear that permanent BMW employees who left the company did so on a *voluntary basis*, always voluntary and always agreed on both sides. So no one could drive the other side, both sides needed to agree.

*DB: Was any of this based on performance at all?*

HK: No, this was quite different. We had a lot of different kinds of cases. For example, sometimes people would say, "I would like to leave," and we would say yes, perhaps we can come to an agreement. Some others said they would like to open their own business, so they would take the severance package and open a business. People who did this came from absolutely different areas of the company. Everyone received a severance package and we were very transparent about this. It was based on how long they had worked for us.

Now you talked about *Leiharbeiter*, the phrase Germans use for contract workers. We call this our "flexible workforce." This was one pillar of our flexibility strategy, but only one pillar. In this way we could reduce a lot of production quickly during the crisis, much earlier than our competitors. In 2008, we had a one-week shutdown in the first week of November, which we don't normally have. In order to avoid producing too many cars we said to our employees, "please take a short holiday, we are closing the plants." Our employees got the same amount of income. We also had short-time working, of course. Then there were the employees on flexible contracts and we were very sorry that we couldn't offer them any more work, but this was part of their employment contract. And even though they didn't work for us anymore, they still remained employed by the contracted company. But on the other hand there's something a lot of people don't talk about: our permanent employees in Germany have great job security. We have a collective agreement with the works council, which protects our employees. So if we have to restructure in some way, close some portion of operations, for example, we offer to absorb those employees into other parts of the company.

*DB: You also pay your "flexible" employees at the same rate as the "tariff" [union contract] employees, isn't that true? It is quite unusual, isn't it?*

HK: Yes, we pay our flexible workforce the same hourly base wage. This was a voluntary agreement my predecessor introduced in 2007 and I think it was a very good idea. It's about treating people fairly and that's why we do it from the very first day.

*DB: I know we are almost out of time but I have one more question: what are the biggest challenges facing you in the HR area in the next two years?*

HK: There are a few things. The first is what I call having the right people in the right place and in the right job for the future. For example, we foresee a limited availability of engineers in the next years. Secondly, what we call "managing competencies." This means going into the phase of plug-in hybrids and other mobility issues, as well as the use of new materials such as carbon fiber.[15] Moving from steel to carbon fiber, this transition means a lot of "managing competencies" and this is where a huge amount of my time is being invested. The third one is demographics: we have an ageing workforce and we need to be more productive at the same time. A fourth one is globalization. For example, we are building a new plant in China and expanding our plants in India and in the States. So we are trying to retain the best people and develop new people there as well. For example, we are setting up a BMW scholar program at our plant in Spartanburg

[South Carolina, USA]. We have a very good apprenticeship program here in Germany, but the US is not as familiar with this. So this is why we will have a program in Spartanburg for apprentices there. We put a new health center in Spartanburg as well. Again, that is something which is driven by how we treat our people, which we believe is the right thing to do, and still cost-effective. Lastly, corporate social responsibility plays an important role at our company and this is definitely something which will be keeping me busy in the future.

*DB: Well, we are done. Thank you so very much!*

As we can see from this interview, BMW is a remarkable organization: not only is it one of the largest and most successful industrial companies in the world, but it has a distinct philosophy that favors its overall workforce, and not just those at the top. It values people, and rewards them based on that value. The benefits of this flowed to BMW after the Crash in spectacular fashion, when the "rebound" effect caused by unprecedented demand from Asia required a level of teamwork that would not have existed at those companies that had "slashed and burned" between 2007 and 2009. BMW demonstrates what happens when the investment in an engaged workforce meets a crisis: the "inoculation" of high engagement prevents the disease that had fatal consequences for others in the same industry. For example, the US's General Motors comes to mind— bankrupted and limping forward as others took market share for a while, before it started its comeback. BMW lives the values, which we have discussed here, brings them to life with its practices, and demonstrates their power.

## Whole Foods Market, Austin, Texas

We have the opportunity to create more conscious and higher trust organizations in the 21st century. To do so will require three major changes: First, the organization must become conscious of its higher purposes. Second, we'll need our leaders to evolve to higher levels of consciousness and trust. Third, we will need to evolve the cultures of our organization(s) in ways that create processes, strategies, and structures that encourage higher levels of trust.[16]
John Mackey, co-founder and co-CEO of Whole Foods Market

Whole Foods Market is the world's largest organic grocer and was founded over 30 years ago in Austin, Texas. The company has operations throughout the United States, and also in Canada and the United Kingdom. Our choice of Whole Foods Market was an easy one: its co-founder and co-CEO, John Mackey, is a high profile individual whose current popularity among hard-core capitalists is somewhat of a paradox, as we shall see. Mr. Mackey is someone who is not afraid to speak his mind and this gives us access to his philosophy and to a better understanding of the basis for his success. Like BMW, Whole Foods takes a stand in favor of its workers, and caps the rewards of its top management in order to balance things across the whole organization. But both companies go much, much further than the area of pay in the respect they pay to their workforce. Like BMW, Whole Foods benefits from this with everything from high engagement to the ultimate recognition that the market can confer: a high share price.

With the Dow Jones Industrial Average™ dipping periodically into and out of negative territory and up only 10% since late October 2010, and this book being written over one year later, Whole Foods is showing a 75–80% increase during this period.[17] It hovers around the all time highs reached in 2005, which is remarkable considering the performance of the overall US market.

As far as its worker engagement levels to which we referred earlier, we note that Whole Foods is one of only 13 companies to have been ranked on *Fortune*'s list of the *100 Best Companies To Work For* in the US since the list's inception.[18]

### Core values at Whole Foods

As one might expect, the culture at Whole Foods is anchored by *core values*, which have to do with stakeholders such as customers, workers, suppliers and the society at large. No doubt, these core values have been a driving force behind Whole Foods' success in the *100 Best Companies To Work For* contest over so many years. Whole Foods lists and details these online, and introduces them with a piece that is well worth reading:[19]

> The following list of core values reflects what is truly important to us as an organization. *These are not values that change from time to time, situation to situation or person to person, but rather they are the underpinning of our company culture.*
>
> Many people feel Whole Foods Market is an exciting company of which to be a part and a very special place to work. These core values are the primary reasons for this feeling, and they transcend our size and our growth rate. By maintaining these core values ... we can preserve what has always been special about our company. *These core values are the soul of our company.*
>
> * Selling the highest quality natural and organic products available
> * Satisfying and delighting our customers
> * Supporting team member happiness and excellence
> * Creating wealth through profits & growth
> * Caring about our communities & our environment
> * Creating ongoing win-win partnerships with our suppliers

- Promoting the health of our stakeholders through healthy eating education

(emphasis added)

The use of the word "happiness" in regard to workers is interesting and increasingly a focus of many organizations. One aspect of this, which Whole Foods details, is what they call "*Shared Fate*": this refers to there being no entitlements in the organization and specifically to their unusual pay equity policy, which we will detail further. We would also point out that the phrase "supporting team member happiness and excellence" is a clever way of stating both that the company *supports an engagement-friendly culture* (e.g., with good management practices) and *recognizes excellent performance* when it occurs.

In 2005 one of us moved to Austin, Texas for a couple of years, and lived down the street from a huge construction project that had just been completed, right in the center of this interesting and lively city.[20] One whole city block had been developed into the new world headquarters of Whole Foods, with a multistory office tower built over what has to be the best-looking and most exciting grocery store (a phrase that is inadequate to describe it) in the world. Whole Foods' flagship store is more an environment than anything else, a place where healthy food is not only sold but also prepared so that one can eat it on-site. At the opening, which we attended, people swarmed the place, TV crews from national networks captured the event and newspapers like *USA Today* soon had multipage color sections dedicated to the store. The widely watched *60 Minutes* news program featured the new store and John Mackey, soon afterwards. We would never have imagined that a grocery store would be a place where one could spend the whole day working (if research and writing is one's profession), but that became the case. With its free wireless network, and an ample supply of great coffee available for purchase, Whole Foods soon became an "office" for many such people, including one of us. This also allowed for long-term observation of employees and how they responded to the many situations that present themselves to workers in the retail business. The impression after some two years was overwhelmingly favorable, indicating that Mr. Mackey had found some answers to the question so many managers and entrepreneurs ask themselves: how do I boost morale and engagement? John Mackey has been sprinkling the blogosphere and other media outlets with his writings and speeches for some time, and it is there that we begin our understanding of how this interesting and successful entrepreneur thinks and operates.

### Understanding the philosophy of Whole Foods' John Mackey: Making capitalism more "conscious"

If you look back at old pictures of the founding of Whole Foods[21] and examine the faces in those pictures (which used to be online but unfortunately are no longer there), it looks like a gathering of hippies. In fact that is exactly what it was, an idealistic move by John Mackey into providing an alternative to what he saw an unhealthy food provided by the established outlets at the time. How Mackey went from hippie-entrepreneur to a darling of the *Wall Street Journal* readers (and investors) is one of those stories that begs to be told.

John Mackey's experience as he became an increasingly successful entrepreneur enabled him to merge some of this idealism into his understanding and interpretation of the capitalist system and combine the two into something quite unusual: *a hybrid capitalism, driven by, as we shall see, all the fervor of a libertarian political mindset, tempered with a highly engagement-friendly philosophy toward his workers.* This was based on a deeply held belief about the capitalist system and its responsibilities: *Mackey was and still is strongly aligned with our view that capitalism is a job- and wealth-creation machine we need to fix, not throw away.* To that end, his goal is to raise the "consciousness" of those in the capitalist system so that its excesses can be tamed while we *all* enjoy its benefits.

What we find refreshing in such an accomplished entrepreneur is that John Mackey is not afraid to take an honest look at the capitalist system and to talk openly about its shortcomings, which surely is the first step in overcoming them. By asking what the true purpose of capitalism is, Mackey gets to the "heart" of the matter. Listen to him as he summarizes where he sees US (although it could be anywhere) society and its woes post-Crash:

> Virtually all of our societal organizations seem to have either forgotten or have never really known why they exist and what their higher purposes are ... Our health care system too often seeks to maximize the profits of pharmaceutical companies, hospitals, doctors, and insurance companies rather than the health and wellness of patients. Many of our corporations primarily exist to maximize the compensation of their executives and, secondarily, shareholder value rather than value creation for customers, employees, and other major stakeholders.[22]

Mackey has expressed these views a number of times, but never as forcefully as in a one-hour interview with an online TV service,[23] which had the time to go into his beliefs in depth and is well worth watching in its entirety. This is especially true if one is both committed to the capitalist system, not blinded to its downsides but also not pessimistic that something can be done to mitigate or change those downsides. We find ourselves squarely in this category, and so to hear John Mackey express it so well is reinforcement indeed. We will summarize its main points here and then take a look at how Mackey's view aligns with many of the points made in this book. First, though, it is important to look at the background against which this interview took place. Understanding that will also shine a strong light onto Mackey's philosophy and values, which in turn drive the culture he has created at Whole Foods Market. This recent background is dominated by a newspaper article he wrote:

### *The Wall Street Journal* "Op-Ed" article and health care at Whole Foods

John Mackey created something of a sensation in the corporate and political world in 2009 when he authored an opinion piece in the highest circulation newspaper in the US, *The Wall Street Journal or WSJ* (owned by Rupert Murdoch's *News Corporation*). In it he took a stand firmly against the proposed Obama health plan and presented the idea that this would be far too much government intervention in health, something which, as a libertarian, he is strongly against. As part of this stand Mackey has created a health benefit at Whole Foods, which offers a very different approach than that offered by President Obama, and which involves a large dose of personal responsibility. This is not easy to do in America, where most who have health insurance have absolutely no idea of the (usually very high) cost of tests, procedures, or even doctor office visits. This is because the private insurance plans provided by their employers, or the Medicare plan for senior citizens, offers no such information, and usually require only *relatively*[24] small co-payments. A change to the law under former President George W. Bush enabled Mackey to bring in a new type of plan in 2003, where employees would be given a high deductible (expenses they would have to meet before the insurance "kicked in") plan along with funds with which they could pay most, but not all, of that deductible. All of these monies would be paid *tax free* into a so-called health savings account, and the key aspect of this was that any funds still in those accounts at year end could be spent by workers on anything they wanted,[25] like normal savings, or simply "rolled over" for future medical expenses! Of course, they could also decide exactly where this money would go during the year on medical tests, procedures and so on. It is easy to imagine that one does not to go the Emergency/Accident department of a hospital with a sniffle when spending one's own money, whereas the incentive to do so when it only costs $20 or less is overwhelming. Mackey wanted to turn his workers into *health care consumers*, not people spending *other people's money* with abandon. Indeed his WSJ article began with a (modified) quote from Margaret Thatcher, which we quote here in its original form:

> Socialist governments traditionally do make a financial mess. They always run out of other people's money.[26]

He explained his plan in detail, showed how it brought worker choice and responsibility to the health care benefit arena, and then pointed out that his workers loved it! Naturally this was his prescription for the whole country, in place of what had quickly become known as *"Obamacare."*

The article, driven from its very beginning by the Thatcher quote, caused tremors among many Whole Foods customers, who complained in droves on the comment pages of the WSJ. How could someone who (they assumed) was so aligned with such liberal things as organic food, animal welfare, corporate greed and so on—John Mackey—turn against his core constituency, the very basis of his customer cohort? How could he turn away from the cherished idea (among many such people) that government should not only be involved in health care but should in fact be the "single payer," à la National Health Service in the UK? A common refrain from such comment writers was that they would "never shop at Whole Foods again!"

If we now fast forward to 2011, it is clear that while Whole Foods might have lost some of these customers, it clearly picked up others whose philosophy aligned with John Mackey's in ways they had perhaps not realized. The 80% stock price rise versus a flatlined Dow Jones Industrial Average underscores this trend. Indeed the comments from many WSJ readers expressed their gleeful discovery of a philosophical soul mate in Mackey, and their desire to take their entire food shopping experience and dollars to Mackey's stores from now on! Given the upscale demographic of WSJ readers, and its overlay with Whole Foods' typical customer,[27] this was a match made in heaven. Whether, on deeper investigation, some of these people found themselves disturbed by Mackey's criticism of corporate "greed" and excessive executive compensation (red meat issues for some WSJ readers, who would disagree with this stance), and whether this would affect their continued presence in his stores, is something we do not yet know.

### The Mackey online TV interview and "conscious capitalism"

Within a couple of months of writing for the WSJ, Mackey was being interviewed by an online TV service backed by a libertarian think tank, and so it is not a surprise that the interview kicks off on this subject. Mackey explains the rising percentage of GDP that health care consumes (4% in 1960 to 17% in 2009), how the new plan at his company in 2003 replaced one that was essentially going bankrupt, and how 90% of his workers never make any claim on the plan, an extraordinary number. When pressed to divulge his political leanings and influences, Mackey does not shy away from admitting to his libertarian views and the influence of Ayn Rand, Adam Smith, John Stuart Mill and especially Ludwig von Mises, the Austrian economist and darling of libertarians.[28] He admits to have voted for a libertarian candidate for President in the 2008 US election. He also defines himself as a *"conscious capitalist,"* and points out that capitalism has done a poor job of branding itself; his point is that after the epic struggle between communism and capitalism in the twentieth century, capitalism failed to capture hearts and minds, often as a result of behavior we have detailed in these pages, such as greed, on which Mackey also focuses in his talks and writings.

"Conscious capitalism" means an increased awareness, and for Mackey this has *four aspects*:

- Business has a broader goal than just making money, and yet many see that as its only goal. Instead "every business is creating value for customers in goods and services, providing jobs for people, providing taxes and donations for communities, outlets for suppliers ... and all those are good things that business and capitalism doesn't get credit for, so we need to articulate that."
- Business is a complex, interdependent system, or Adam Smith's "harmony of interest;" if we start at the worker level, this means managers doing their job to train and create conditions in which these workers are happy, which then leads to happy customers and that in turn leads to happy shareholders. In other words, Mackey's vision aligns perfectly with our model of engagement, customer satisfaction and organization performance we detailed earlier. For Whole Foods, this is "harmony of interest" in action.
- Capitalism's "brand" is greatly harmed by executives taking "hundreds of millions of dollars." When pressed as to whether they are not "worth it," Mackey responds that this is a "rigged game" and that the market really has little to do with it. As one would expect, though, his prescription is not government intervention but a raising of consciousness in this area, something which, as we write, appears to be underway.[29]

At this point in the interview,[30] Mackey makes what is a central point in this book:

> I think an organization has to think not only about external equity but also about internal equity, what everyone else in the organization is making, *and you have to balance that out.*
>
> (emphasis added)

Mackey "walks the talk" with these principles at Whole Foods by making every effort to not appear as a greedy capitalist, by taking only $1 a year in salary, and as we have seen by controlling the maximum pay ratio internally for others (19:1). He does not suffer financially, of course, as the founder of a successful business and a holder of a lot of its stock, estimated at $80 million as of the time of writing. But as he points out, he has clearly avoided squeezing every drop of cash out of this company, and this aligns with the third principle of conscious capitalism, mentioned before. He believes that this is good for morale, and we agree with him.

- Demonstrating that, like most important concepts, conscious capitalism is a work in progress, Mackey adds a *fourth aspect* at a later date in another interview:

> And the fourth principle of conscious capitalism is that you have to create a culture that supports purpose, stakeholders, and leadership, so that it all fits together.[31]

It is interesting that this was added some two years after the interview from which we collected the first three principles. It is not enough to talk about these things and their importance in the work environment. They need to be implemented, made real, and the only way to do that is to review and change all aspects of the work culture to align with them, exactly as we have suggested in Chapter 4.

## Where John Mackey, Whole Foods and Ayn Rand part company (fortunately)

It is striking to hear that John Mackey studied Ayn Rand and voted for a libertarian candidate for President of the United States at the last election. This would seem to place him squarely among those who have been huge fans of *Atlas Shrugged* (both the book and the somewhat awkward film that was recently made from the book) and Ms. Rand's underlying principle, which we have examined earlier, that self-interest is the highest moral value. This would have disqualified him from being featured in a book with the subtitle *"Balancing Me and We"* for sure! But Mackey cannot be pigeon-holed this way; he is what we might call a cafeteria-libertarian, taking something from here and something from there but not buying into any one overriding approach. Fortunately, in our opinion, he goes strongly against what we might call "unbridled self-interest." Listen to his words on a blog featured on the WF web site, in a piece titled *"Defending the Morality of Capitalism"*[32]:

> What I'm suggesting is that human beings are complex and we have many motivations, of which self-interest is one, but hardly the only one. We're motivated by many things that we care about, that include, but are not limited to, our self-interest. I think that in some ways the libertarian movement—*possibly due to the combined influence of Ayn Rand and many economists—has gotten to a kind of ideological dead end* that I don't think does justice to business or capitalism or human nature.

> (emphasis added)

Just as he stepped out of his hippie past and into the role of the *Wall Street Journal* superstar, Mackey here steps out of the libertarian straightjacket and into a much more compassionate and broad-based interpretation of what society needs from capitalism. In doing so he has become someone of significant value on the world stage right at this moment, someone who is actually helping to move capitalism forward and make it work for everyone.

### Understanding the philosophy of John Mackey: Executive compensation at Whole Foods

Mackey's view on executive pay is *conscious capitalism in action*. In terms of US practices, it is well outside the current mainstream, but may be a harbinger of the future. His views have been expressed in an important blog post that gets to the heart of how Mackey sees his business and its relationship with the workers who make it run. It appeared in the Harvard Business Review Blog in June 2009 and was titled *"Why Sky-High CEO Pay is Bad Business."*[33] How many other CEOs would write such a piece that would argue against their own apparent self-interest? Only those who understand that their "self-interest" might in fact be enhanced if they broaden their perspective to include as many others in their organization as possible. How many would have the courage to face up to a problem that revolves around their own pay, *and then actually solve it* in their organization? Both *talk and then walk the talk*? We have the answer: *very, very few, if any*. Without putting the man on the virtual couch, perhaps the idealistic hippie in Mackey never died off, but remained as a moral compass inside the increasingly successful (and wealthy) CEO. How refreshing!

Mackey begins his blog discussion with a look at the history of executive compensation in the US, using data we have shared earlier in this book. The extraordinary climb from the 1960s to now is documented, and an effective push-back is made against theories saying that this is "market driven." Then Mackey makes the statement that underscores his qualification for inclusion here:

> Because of the yawning gap between the leaders and the led, employee morale is suffering, talented performers' loyalty is evaporating, and strategy and execution is suffering at American companies.

Here we have the argument in one brief statement: the *"gap between the leaders and the led,"* the one that disqualifies those leaders from being able to stand up and honestly say *"we're all in this together."*

Whole Foods, via John Mackey's leadership, has always been mindful of this gap and has done something practical to address it: some 22 years ago, when this issue was not in the public eye nearly as much as it is now, the company had actually set the maximum ratio of CEO (or any other executive) to average Whole Foods worker pay at 8:1. At that time, sales were $40 million a year. In 2009, with sales at $8 billion, the ratio had worked its way up to 19:1 and remains at that level today, still a far, far cry from the US averages of 300–450:1, which we have seen. The first question that comes to mind, and one that Mackey surely must get with every interview on this subject, is whether this pay cap has either prevented the company from hiring top quality managers or made it lose good people from the management ranks. Mackey states that

> Whole Foods has never lost to a competitor a top executive that we wanted to keep since the company began more than 30 years ago.

While not covering our first question, this is interesting. Mackey explains it by saying that in the hierarchy of needs at work, pay is relatively less important. In doing so he does indeed align himself with what we have found in countless surveys. One of the reasons for this is that, under most normal economic conditions and in most industrialized countries, pay has to be competitive just to get people to work at a given organization. Once there, other factors, especially the key relationship with the manager and the nature of the work itself, then become much more important day to day.

By setting a numeric target for the CEO to average worker pay ratio, Whole Foods appears to be almost unique among the larger US companies, although that information is not always readily available. Recent changes in US government regulation will make the disclosure of this ratio mandatory among companies that are publicly traded, although stockholders currently seem to be less concerned about this than they should be.[34] We believe it will become more important, in time, perhaps as the public becomes more and more fed up with inequalities in the workplace, and realize the reality that CEO pay and performance are often barely related. "Proactive" companies like Whole Foods are way ahead of this curve and we believe they will benefit from this approach with all their stakeholders.

### How Whole Foods achieves high engagement with workers, and customers

Everything we have seen so far about co-CEO John Mackey's philosophy has been woven into the culture of Whole Foods over the 30+ years that the company has been in existence. Since it is far easier to write and talk about such lofty ideals than actually make them happen, this is a significant achievement. But aside from the executive pay to worker pay ratio in place for many years, how, specifically, does Mackey bring his philosophy to life on a day-to-day basis? We will examine several areas and use his own words to describe this:

- Making the core values real for workers

> One of the most important parts of my job is touring our stores and talking to our Team Members, customers, and suppliers. I know that in

virtually everything that I say and do, our Team Members are always studying me, trying to determine whether they can trust me and the mission of the company. I'm always on stage. So walking the talk is very important. I try to communicate the mission and values of Whole Foods Market at every opportunity and I try to live those core values myself with complete fidelity. Fidelity to the mission and values builds trust, while any deviation from these ideals undermines trust. High trust organizations and hypocritical leadership are mutually exclusive.[35]

- Aligning Whole Foods' values with its customer and worker base
The organic and natural food business is one that has its share of demanding and value-driven customers, who are often served by Whole Foods workers whose knowledge and values align with those of their customers; the workers' passion for healthy food drives their desire to work in that particular field. One can therefore easily imagine that things like animal welfare, fair trade, sustainability and related issues would be front and center for both workers and customers. This is indeed the case and has, for example, resulted in a comprehensive (and no doubt costly) effort to "rate" each animal product on a 1–5 scale. This is called the *5-Step™ Animal Welfare Rating Standards.*[36]

  John Mackey believes that we have moved from a stage in human development when cost was the only consideration for food, to the point where every aspect of food production is now examined by consumers,[37] which includes the welfare of animals, the welfare of workers who produce the food, the environmental impact and so on.[38]

- Trust is not a one-way street

  Many leaders make the mistake of believing that the key to increasing organizational trust is to somehow get the workforce to trust the leadership more. While it is very important that employees trust leadership, it is equally important that the leadership trust the workforce. To receive trust, it is usually necessary that we give trust.[39]

- Empowerment
As we have seen, this word is one of the most widely used and poorly implemented in our organizations. As Mackey points out, one of the reasons for this is the way in which management still clings to power and control:

  The effectiveness of teams is tremendously enhanced when they are fully empowered to do their work and to fulfill the organization's mission and values. Empowerment must be much, much more than a mere slogan, however. It should be within the very DNA of the organization. Empowerment unleashes creativity and innovation and rapidly accelerates the evolution of the organization. Empowered organizations have tremendous competitive advantage because they have tapped into levels of energy and commitment which their competitors usually have difficulty matching. Nothing holds back empowerment more than the leadership philosophy of command and control.[40]

- Fairness
  We have placed great emphasis on this word and its value when made part of the high engagement culture. Mackey aligns with our view:

  Nothing unravels trust more quickly in an organization than either the reality or the perception of unfairness. Another important virtue of creating a culture of transparency is that it helps ensure that unfairness is clearly seen and can therefore be corrected quickly. It is essential that the ethic of fairness apply to all key organizational processes such as hiring, promotion, compensation, discipline, and termination. Favoritism and nepotism undermine organizational trust.[41]

- "Creating a culture of love and care"
  Mackey is not afraid to use a word such as "love" in his writings. In his view of the work environment, this is something that is missing, as organizations strive to be "tougher" than the competition, and "driven" to success by their internal culture. In his view, perhaps borrowed from the spiritual text, *A Course in Miracles*, love is the opposite of fear, and fear is a killer of most good things in an organization, *especially morale and engagement*. Many of us can attest to the reality of that, although some fear can be valuable: fear of losing market share or being overtaken technologically can be a positive motivating force. Day-to-day fear of one's boss, of losing one's job, of favoritism-based rather than performance-based decisions affecting us, these are another matter.

  Mackey proposes that decisions about promotions, for example, should consider the "love and care" that an individual can bring to the job, not just technical prowess, something we have already endorsed, although not in these words. Similarly, creating a culture of forgiveness rather than condemnation forms part of his approach; people are still held accountable but are coached and mentored rather than condemned when they make mistakes. Recognition, which we have discussed as an increasing focus of many successful organizations, forms a big part of the Mackey and Whole Foods universe.

## BMW and Whole Foods Market: Showing us the way forward

Whether one is in the business of bending metal (or, increasingly, spinning out carbon fiber) to make automobiles or selling organic groceries or meats from humanely-treated animals, the principles of a high-engagement work culture remain the same. These principles are what we believe are necessary in these difficult times. BMW and Whole Foods show us that putting "we," in the form of their stakeholders (and especially their workers) ahead of "me" (especially top management income and interests), is a profitable and successful strategy. This is a "conscious" and successful form of capitalism that happens to be aligned with huge trends happening in the world today. Why we should all be moving in this direction in our organizations is something we will now examine.

# 6
## Why All This Matters So Much, and Where We Go From Here

The Middle Class Is Too Big To Fail

Banner seen at an *Occupy Wall Street* demonstration, October 2011, echoing the phrase used in the 2008 bail-out of large US banks deemed too important and large to be allowed to "go under"

Something very, very big is happening as we write this book: a political movement is stirring, starting on Wall Street but probably inspired by the sheer power and courage of the *Arab Spring*.[1] It is moving not just around the United States (in 200+ locations), but overseas: London, Paris, Madrid, Rome, Frankfurt—all have been inspired to stand up and make a statement. *Is this the beginning of a worldwide evolution—or revolution?* It is far too early to tell. What does it have to do with what we are talking about in this book? As we will see, some of it has quite a lot in common. Other parts of the protests come with messages with which we would strongly disagree.

When one looks at the banners carried by the protestors, there is a wide range of subject matter, but one topic comes up the most frequently: *the 99% and the 1%.* This refers to the concentration of wealth in the US, where the top 1% controls some 36% of the wealth, a number that (unlike during the Great Depression) *increased* since the Crash.[2] As we write, data appears that gives powerful support to the protestors: according to the non-partisan Congressional Budget Office (CBO), the income of the top 1% of US individuals had increased by 275% from 1979 to 2007. For the top 20%, there was a 65% increase, while for the bottom quintile, that number is 18% in the same period.[3] The report says that one of the main factors in this surge at the top is, as we have discussed, the arms race in *executive compensation.* Doubtless other countries' protestors have their own 1% "issue" as well. As our previous reference points out, the Great Depression was a powerful wealth-leveling mechanism, which endured for a long time. Combined with other factors such as US union activity, and the spread of communism elsewhere, pressures toward a more equitable sharing of wealth were intense. With the fall of communism in 1989, there is no such external pressure, but the demonstrations tell us that other mechanisms, such as the effects of the Crash, are now at work. *The 99% is waking up*, which is the reason for something we frequently see in the hands of the demonstrators, the banners with the word *"WE"* prominently highlighted: a word that is a key focus of this book.

In references to the bailout of Wall Street during the Crash, protestors chant: *"Banks Got Bailed Out, We Got Sold Out!"* We have previously discussed one aspect of this with the phrase *"privatized profits and socialized losses."* That this is happening should not be surprising; the only surprise is the delay in reaction, because the after-effects of the Crash have been with us now for over three years. Unemployment remains high in the US and Europe is staggering from one precipice to another as it tries to decide if richer countries should bail out poorer (and more profligate) ones. As all this grinds on for years, people lose their patience and their hope that things will soon change, and this breaks out into demonstrations. Witness the downfall of President Obama's favorability ratings, riding high (around 70% favorable) on words like "hope" and "change" after his election, and now at close to his lowest levels (39%).[4] Will the Crash cause him to be a one-term President? The odds now are now about 50:50 that the answer is "yes."[5]

## Why this all matters so much

Our thesis in this book is that change is necessary in our organizations, not to mention elsewhere, and we believe that these events are a sign that that change is beginning. Ultimately, people will not stand for extremes of unfairness and lack of accountability at both the societal and organizational levels, especially when they get stuck with the bill. They will not stand for certain companies holding us hostage and threatening our very way of life and standard of living. For us, the US *Tea Party* and *Occupy Wall Street* are two sides of the same coin, expressing many of the same feelings, albeit it from different sides of the political spectrum and with somewhat different solutions. At the core of their sense of unfairness in society is an intense frustration with the status quo that holds this in place. Is this really any different, albeit it on another level, from the feelings expressed in the *Arab Spring*? Given the powers aligned behind the status quo, however, we need to corral and sharpen our arguments and voice our demands such that the push for change is irresistible. As we have seen, the Crash had both governmental and organizational aspects to it: the governmental ones (changes in regulation such as allowing extreme levels of leverage and the dismantling of a "firewall" between retail and investment banking activities) had been put in place after ferocious lobbying. The lobbyists are still in place and unlikely to give up years of gains without a fight. In the United States alone lobbying of politicians brought in some $3.5 *billion* in 2010 and is on track to repeat this in 2011.[6] That is why some say that America has the best government that money can buy! Not only the *Occupy Wall Street* protestors, but the larger American public is fed up with this situation: in a poll reported on a cable TV station, some 86% of respondents (from a sample that reflected the total US population) reported that "*Wall Street has too much power in Washington D.C.*"[7] Imagine if football were run like this: each game fixed by the "vested interests." No one would attend or watch on TV. The game would be destroyed by its own corruption.

To counter these forces of resistance and thinly veiled patronage (and not just in the US!) we are actually *lucky* to be living in such turbulent times: we believe that the pressure created by the Crash will be so intense that things will not just settle back into what they were. The Wall Street banks did not know it at the time but they have created a movement of tectonic proportions and the plates have moved. This is like when India crashed into its future continental partner, Eurasia, and slowly formed the Himalayas! In this new, fertile landscape we can see the "green shoots" of new growth. Should we expect otherwise in a universe that seems to constantly rearrange itself, which has utter contempt for the "status quo"?

Let's remind ourselves why we need fundamental change, *and what is at stake here for our organizations*, by looking at just three after-effects of the Crash:

- *Disengagement of workers*: As we have seen, morale and engagement in many countries around the world is quite low. The Crash has made this worse, with unemployment high, job security much lower and mobility between jobs often curtailed. People are "stuck," the job markets are frozen. How many hundreds of thousands or millions of workers are just biding their time in the "wrong" job, with the "wrong" boss because they cannot escape? How does this affect productivity? It is huge, incalculable. The Crash is to blame for a significant part of this.
- *Destruction of Western competitive edge*: The Crash was a distinctly Western affair. If you are reading this in Asia, especially in China, you know you have been handed a gift, from which you will benefit enormously. If you are in the West, especially the US, you will see the effects of this gift for generations. From a stunning 11.9% growth rate in the year before the Crash, in 2007, China dipped to "only" about 9% in 2008 and 2009, the most severe years of the Crash for Western economies and most others in Asia. In 2010 it climbed above 10% again[8] and is humming along quite well in 2011, at an estimated 9%, according to the World Bank.[9] These are incredible numbers and contrast with the staggering state of China's competition in that same period: the Crash has left behind massive damage in economies from

the US to Greece and Italy. In a 2010 article in *The Wall Street Journal*, Niall Ferguson suggests that

> Nothing is more certain to accelerate the shift of global economic power from West to East than the looming U.S. fiscal crisis. With a debt-to-revenue ratio of 312%, Greece is in dire straits already. But the debt-to-revenue ratio of the U.S. is 358%, according to Morgan Stanley. The Congressional Budget Office estimates that interest payments on the federal debt will rise from 9% of federal tax revenues to 20% in 2020, 36% in 2030 and 58% in 2040.[10]

In case we think that the West can compete because of its powerhouse intellectual property, even as it loses manufacturing, China overtook Germany in patents in 2007. Patent applications in 2008 for China, India, South Korea and Japan exceeded those from the West for the first time.[11] Clearly, we can no longer hide behind the wall of "innovation" as we recover from the Crash. The question is, as we stated at the beginning of this book, can we afford to shoot ourselves in the foot in this way more than once? While the US debt pile did not all occur during the Crash, but had been the result of profligate spending by both major political parties going back decades, the Crash made things much worse. Competitors are not standing still.

- *Disillusion with capitalism:* Who can blame people from being angry with the capitalist system? Who can blame them for wanting something different, even though they know from recent history that other models are even worse? This is unfortunate but understandable because while there are some John Mackeys out there trying their hardest to build a new model of capitalism that works for "we," there are more who seem to want to move in the other direction, who work hard every day to perpetuate an unfair, "me"-based system. In turn, government reacts to popular outrage with more and more heavy-handed regulation, which is sure to make things worse for everyone.

## Where we go from here

The effects of the Crash go beyond this, we know that we could write about how greed has been rewarded and so on, but the previous list is surely significant enough. It can depress us, or motivate us—and we choose the latter. Since our mandate here is, thankfully, to focus on organizational solutions, we can skip fairly lightly over areas like government reform, tax reform, etc. while pointing out that they are necessary and relevant in countries across the world. In doing so we note that in those areas the push-back is not coming just from the protestors on Wall Street, but also from some who have benefitted the most from capitalism's success. Listen to one of the richest men in America and a famed investor, Warren Buffett. He knows what is happening, because he is a beneficiary:

> [T]here's class warfare, all right ... But it's my class, the rich class, that's making war, and we're winning.[12]

Buffett is famous for pointing out that his tax rate, at 15%,[13] is extremely unfair when compared to that of his secretary, whose marginal rate is 26.5%.[14,15] Buffett has a net worth of about $45 billion.[16]

John Bogle, the founder of the Vanguard Funds and another famed investment guru and pillar of the capitalist establishment, finds himself quite disillusioned with the whole system: in his 2005 book, *Battle for the Soul of Capitalism*, Bogle warned us the "Invisible Hand" (of Adam Smith) no longer serves "We the People" or the public welfare. We would argue that Smith's invisible hand has been replaced by the equally invisible hand of lobbyists. Bogle went as far as to declare the *Death of Capitalism*, a pessimistic view with which we do not agree, although we note that his comment was very prescient in foreseeing today's events.

While tax codes and other mechanisms need to be adjusted in certain countries to allow for a more level economic playing field, the issue of how to create a fairer and more "we"-friendly form of capitalism is something our organizations can do by themselves. Allowing them to find the path to a "better way of doing things," *instead of turning to more government regulation*, is a fundamental belief we bring to this book. In most developed countries there are already very strict rules in place as to how business should operate. Some of these, like laws concerning fraud, have been in place since Roman times![17] The issue is whether these are applied, and as we have noted, no one has gone to jail in the US for any reason as a result of the Crash, in spite of what most agree is widespread criminal activity. With this in mind and our previous comments from Professor Enderby about the dangers of regulating capitalism's animal spirits to death, we look for bold organizational solutions to these issues, like those we have seen at BMW and Whole Foods. When we look in that direction, we see solutions that apply a broad brush and those that are very focused, like our fairer and more engagement-friendly workplace culture driven by the **BEST** *practices*, which apply at the organizational level. The common element to both approaches is that they push back against the "me" forces, (*without trying to destroy them*) and *balance them* with more "we." Both approaches are two sides of the same coin, meaning that changes to the way we reinvent capitalism to work more for the greater good can only be realized at individual organizations. Let's look first at a macro approach that relates to the core thesis in this book.

### The macro view: Michael Porter and "Shared Value"

Michael Porter is a well-known Harvard Professor and major contributor to thought in the area of management and strategy. His paper called *"Creating Shared Value"*[18] appeared in the *Harvard Business Review* (HBR) early in 2011 and has some powerful ideas that will not seem unfamiliar, following our examination of the philosophy of John Mackey in the previous chapter. Porter begins by echoing the Mackey theme that business is being blamed for many of society's ills, certainly something that the *Occupy Wall Street* protestors would affirm. Porter looks back through history and sees a damaging trend from a time when companies were much more "rooted" in their local communities, and acted in those communities' best interests, to a present when outsourcing, downsizing and short-term focus only on profit has significantly eroded their stature in society. For Porter, there is often little to show in a given community where a company is located, even as profits rise; instead communities often see profits coming at their expense. Porter points out that this and other effects of business' isolation often results in government intervention, which makes such businesses less competitive than before, thereby creating a downward spiral. This works against the reality of the absolute dependency that society and business have for each other. What is interesting, though, is that he places most of the blame squarely on the shoulders of business, not government. Listen to him as he describes what happens as companies attempt to create value, but do so in a bubble, ignoring the state in which many of their stakeholders find themselves:

> How else could companies overlook the well-being of their customers, the depletion of natural resources vital to their businesses, the viability of key suppliers, or the economic distress of the communities in which they produce and sell? How else could companies think that simply shifting activities to locations with ever lower wages was a sustainable "solution" to competitive challenges?[19]

We would add to that list, *the well-being of their workers*, although he has alluded to that in the last sentence quoted before. He then goes on to make a very interesting statement:

> Companies must take the lead in bringing business and society back together.[20]

Our readers will be very familiar with the field of *corporate social responsibility*, or CSR, which has exploded in recent years. Porter points out that this is not a warmed-over version of CSR, but a whole new approach: the difference is that, in his view, CSR approaches the organization's social responsibilities as *peripheral issues* outside its core mission. For Porter, *creating shared value is part of the core mission.* That is, success must be measured not only in terms of quarterly financial results within the "bubble" of the organization but also *how the larger society is doing as a result of that organization's activities.* When Porter places CSR and Shared Value side by side, he notes that CSR often comes about as a result of external pressure, while Shared Value is "integral to competing;" CSR is quite separate from profit maximization, while Shared Value is also integral to that. Shared Value differentiates itself from CSR by *not* being the following:

- Redistribution of corporate wealth, in activities like the "fair trade" movement with coffee farmers: A Shared Value approach would be to help growers increase yields and improve growing techniques instead, not just to pay higher prices for their coffee. Instead of redistribution, Shared Value looks to *"expand the pool of economic and social value."*[21]
- Charity: Shared Value's goal is greater benefit for all participants in the chain, not a handout or some other form of philanthropy to burnish the organization's image.
- Shared personal "values": Something we have discussed previously in connection with workplace culture.

Porter is scathing in his analysis of the Crash. Listen to him describe the role of US banks and the thinly disguised alibi of Social Responsibility behind which they tried to hide, after the fact:

> [The banks] promoted unsustainable financing vehicles that turned out to be socially and economically devastating, while claiming they were socially responsible because they had charitable contribution programs.[22]

Shared Value appeals to us because it is not anticapitalism; *Shared Value is firmly in the capitalist camp. It merely extends that camp beyond the limited borders of each individual organization.* Shared Value seeks a positive benefit (including financial outcome) for all stakeholders, from the organization itself to the broader society of which it is part.

In the economic world view made famous by the University of Chicago Nobel Prize Winner Milton Friedman, business does good by providing jobs, paying taxes and so on. It has no role outside that one, *even including a role limited to CSR,* of which Friedman was quite critical.[23] Clearly, Shared Value goes much, much further than Friedman's view and CSR, and argues for much deeper connections into society, not out of a sense of obligation, guilt, image building or other superficial motives but *because the organization will benefit enormously by doing so.*

If we give an example of Starbucks Coffee Company, an organization many love and some hate (mostly those who regret the loss of small, independent coffee houses), it would have satisfied the Friedman perspective simply to be creating so many jobs and paying all the taxes, occupying all the square footage in shopping malls around the world and so on. But founder and CEO Howard Schultz went much further, focusing on his employees and the culture in which they would work from day one. This has been the reason that in the US many thousands, probably hundreds of thousands, of single mothers have found work there and supported their families because of the health benefits for part-time workers that Schultz provided, unlike almost any other large US business. This cost serious money but Starbucks has been a spectacular success in the US (and later worldwide). Shared Value would say that many of these grateful workers became customers, talked up Starbucks to friends who also became customers, etc. Our understanding of Schultz's motives would have us believe that he did not make this move for that reason, even if that was its outcome. He made the move because he believed in the "greater good." A "virtuous circle" was created, exactly as Porter suggests. Society benefited, Starbucks benefited.

We note here that *Shared Value does not require a benevolent or altruistic mind-set*: one can be a hard-core and driven capitalist and implement Shared Value, *simply because it drives performance*. As Porter says:

There is nothing soft about Shared Value.[24]

We find this argument compelling and it is exactly the one we have made about morale and engagement in *Employee Morale*: you don't have to be "touchy-feely" to focus on morale or engagement, it is so effective at driving performance that you can push for it even if you do not have one "touchy-feely" bone in your body.[25,26]

The approach before Shared Value, where the business had to succeed in order to have *something left over* for more altruistic activities beneficial to society, was the basis for a common phrase we have often heard:

You've got to do well to do good.

Shared Value appears to put this on its head:

If you want to do *really, really* well, do good!

We recognize the arguments Porter makes here; they dovetail well with what we have been saying throughout this book. They are about *the balance between "me" and "we,"* with "me" as the isolated, inward looking and increasingly short term-oriented business, and "we" as the society at large, certainly a broader definition of "stakeholders" than one usually finds. Signs are every-where (including many in Porter's article) that this vision, this framework for a "better way of doing things" is starting to be implemented. Here are some examples.

*Shared Value in action: The example of India*

In a fascinating article in the August 2011 edition of *HR Magazine*,[27] which was adapted from a book on Indian business by Peter Cappelli, professor of management at the University of Pennsylvania's Wharton School and director of Wharton's Center for Human Resources,[28] the author lays out some informa-tion on the goals and values of Indian business that align perfectly with what we have been discussing here. Cappelli and his co-authors interviewed many of the CEOs of India's biggest companies and found out that

> Indian business leaders are deeply involved in solving societal problems. They deem it entirely appropriate to do so; *they describe the purpose of their companies as addressing social issues.*[29]

> (emphasis added)

Cappelli points out that some of this focus comes from the Hindu culture, but goes beyond that by placing *national purpose* above financial gain. What he calls the "India Way" is characterized by, among other things, a focus on *"holis-tic engagement" of workers*[30] and this sense of *social purpose* that is at the core of Shared Value. All of this is contrasted in the article with the US's overwhelming focus on "shareholder value," and placed in the context of India barely slowing down during the "Great Recession." Shared Value works!

*Building on the vision of Shared Value: Hiring and training workers*

Peter Cappelli has extended his support of this approach in one of the most commented articles in recent weeks in *The Wall Street Journal*, which appeared as we were writing this book. In an article titled *"Finding the Right Employees,"*[31] he makes some startling observations and provides a prescription for change, which is straight out of the Shared Value vision. He points out that there are simply too many people[32] being rejected for jobs for which they would be very capable, and gives the example of one company that had 25,000 applications for a job but did not find the person they were looking for in that group! What was the missing ability? Walking on water? Often, Cappelli observes, comput-ers sift through resumes and when they do not find the exact "fit," they reject. One individual was told that he was perfect for a job but was rejected because the *title of his previous job was not exactly that of the new job*! Professor Cappelli has a field day in his criticism, and rightly so. His main point is a powerful one: unlike in other countries, the US provides a pitiful level of training and apprenticeship programs that will prepare people for jobs and help them once they get those jobs. Many US organizations have completely given up doing much in-house, but they then turn around and blame the education system for not giving them exactly what they want. Cappelli demolishes this argument by showing that this is not the place for blame, and that US companies should start to function more like their European counterparts (as much as some might find that distasteful!), by supporting extensive apprenticeship and in-house training efforts. BMW would be a good place to look at how well this works. This benefits society as a whole and ultimately provides all the advantages promised by Shared Value.

*Building on the vision of Shared Value: Meeting new generational needs and values*

Michael Porter has a viewpoint about younger generations of managers-to-be, which builds on our example of Harvard Business School earlier in the book, when we saw that Dean Nitin Nohria was shifting the curriculum more toward *ethics and teamwork*. The Dean also accepted the fact that some of his graduates played a role in the Crash. Porter would appear to agree with Dean Nohria in terms of the need to shift the focus of B-school study, as reflected in these comments from the Shared Value article about the next generation of customers and managers:

> The moment for a new conception of capitalism is now; society's needs are large and growing, while ... a new generation of young people are asking business to step up ... Most business schools still teach the narrow view of capitalism, even though more and more of their graduates hunger for a greater sense of purpose and a growing number are drawn to social entrepreneurship. The results have been missed opportunity and public cynicism.[33]

We would add to this that we hope the idealism of the students to which Porter refers remains in place, unlike that of some of the previous generations, whose idealistic past lead to an extremely egoistic consumer-oriented future and created many of the problems that caused the Crash! There are also risks of going too far "back": the large cohort that we have examined before, the Millennials (born 1978–2000) seem like they will favor more government intervention, as a push-back to "big business," as we see here:

> Millennials, more so than other generations, want a stronger government to make the economy work better, help those in need, and provide more services. They decisively reject the conservative viewpoint that government is the problem, and that free markets always produce the best results for society; instead they support a more balanced approach to the economy.[34]

They need to be convinced that government is not always the best vehicle for providing things, and that a capitalist system that works for everyone (as in Shared Value and our BMW and Whole Foods examples) could well do a better job.

## Conclusion

### Toward a fairer, "happier," more engaged work culture, which works for everyone

We began this book with the Crash, its causes and effects. We argued that our organizations had something very significant to do with it and because of that *we had a chance to do things differently.* Our journey took us through the whole area of culture and engagement to ego and its corrosive effects on organizational (and regular!) life. We presented a way to build something at the organizational level, which met our criteria for *building the high engagement culture.*

Throughout this book, our focus has been on moving toward a balance of "me" and "we" in our organizations, and doing so while maintaining the capitalist system that is the only one that can drive a modicum of well-being for the majority of the seven billion people now on this planet.[35,36] As flawed as it is, capitalism is the survivor of a fierce ideological competition that ended in 1989 with the collapse of a far more corrupt, damaging[37] and dangerous ideology from which its unwilling participants often tried to flee. At the same time as it supports this imperfect but fixable system, our approach has had a key goal of preserving individual initiative and motivation *while stressing the "greater good" as a goal for our organizations*. It delivers something for which most of us hunger in life in general and especially at work: *fairness*. Conservatives and liberals, socialists and libertarians, can get behind the value of fairness; it is a politically agnostic idea. As we have stressed over and over (because it is a critical issue), it does not mean that everyone has an equal outcome, and we continually push back against those who wish to hijack the concept of fairness and tar it with the brush of "equality." On the contrary, *fairness ensures ongoing competition, and rewards true performance, whether at the individual or group level*.

So can we achieve all this, or is it all a fantasy world? We believe strongly that we can, as we demonstrated in our case studies. We believe that we must, that ultimately our standard of living, worldwide, depends on it. But not just that, there is something else that might just be equally—or more—important: *our happiness*.

It seems strange to talk about being "happy" at a time when people seem to be anything but that. But we believe that when life becomes difficult that is actually a great time to look for a "better way of doing things." Are people in many Western countries, and even those in the East, "barking up the wrong tree" when it comes to their goals and aspirations, *their very way of life*? In the

US, there is much hand-wringing about the fact that, for the first time, the next generation will not have a "better life" than the current post-World War II "baby boomers." But is this realistic, and in any case, what does a "better life" consist of? More McDonalds stores to visit? Even faster and better computers and other communications devices? In other words, it is typically seen in *material terms*. Is all of this making us any happier? It depends on whom you ask: a survey of international happiness conducted by, of all places, North Korea, showed that China was the happiest country in the world followed by—of course—North Korea. Of course, the archenemy of North Korea, the US, was bottom of the list.[38] This underscores the fact that one should choose one's survey company carefully! More typical is the list that shows Denmark or another Nordic country as the happiest in the world, although lists vary in what they include. *Often, there is no strong correlation between material wealth and happiness.* For example, one list from the New Economics Foundation in 2009 shows the US in 114th place and the UK in 74th, worldwide, with Costa Rica as number one.[39] The University of Michigan's *World Values Surveys* for 2008 show Puerto Rico at number one, the US at 15 and Germany at 25.[40] Typical variables measured include a combination of economic factors along with social issues and individual emotional states, although obviously those combinations vary greatly by source. The International Institute of Management points out that in 2005:

> The independent London-based think tank New Economics Foundation (NEF) [was] pushing for the implementation of a set of national well-being accounts that would tote up life satisfaction and personal development, as well as issues such as trust and engagement. The accounts would also include liabilities, such as stress and depression.[41]

What is especially interesting is that serious-minded people such as economists have ventured into the field of national happiness, given that they cannot predict human economic development and behavior without this "X" factor. It became clear that happier people were more productive than unhappy ones:

> The answer is simple: mental and emotional well-being of citizens improves their performance and broadens the intellectual, physical and social resources of a nation.[42]

How interesting: if we focus on happiness, *we do not have to lose our competitive edge or our standard of living, in fact we might actually enhance it!*

The idea that a state could and should focus in this area dates back to 1972 and the remote Asian country of Bhutan, which has now become famous for being the first to have done so. The then King (HM Jigme Singye Wangchuck) rightly pointed out that there is more to life than *Gross National Product* and suggested *Gross National Happiness* as an adjunct. Signs appear in Bhutan schools that GNH is more important than GNP![43] Should we all be listening to this little country with the higher purpose? We believe so, and that our organizations can and should be playing a central role as we try to do more than recover from the Crash, as we try to move in a new, *fairer direction that works for everyone.* They can play this role by making every effort to create the conditions in which workers engage, and by extending their role in society beyond the limited focus that has recently been the case for so many. *Surely, happiness, both at work and outside it, depends in good part on this?* If that is not enough to convince, or if "happiness" is too soft a goal for some in spite of the real-world benefits we have described, we would point out that capitalism itself may also be at stake, if it continues to threaten the financial underpinnings of society by pandering to its greedy side. *"Business as usual" is not an option.* Just as the "99%" seem to be waking up, capitalism itself needs to wake up and see reality. Moving in a new direction can salvage its reputation and re-establish a groundswell of support for itself.

### Positivism versus pessimism

As we write, the Crash that Ben Bernanke of the US Federal Reserve described as *"worse than the Great Depression"* has ground us down for three years. It's hard to keep a positive outlook when the nightly newscasts show long lines of unemployed people trying to get the few jobs that are available, when work-places have become so short-term results orientated, when more people are working longer hours, and are feeling increasingly that they have less control and autonomy at work. But we need to push back against this pessimism, to create a different, more engaging, more people-friendly set of work environments, with greater camaraderie, fun and motivation. Environments that draw their inspiration and strength from *the extraordinary experience of being alive here, on this planet, spinning through space.* More often than not, that experience is something we take for granted, and so we need reminders: perhaps we need an "awakening" experience at work akin to Leonard's experience (played by Robert de Niro) in the film *Awakenings* (1990). He reads a newspaper for the first time after many years in a catatonic state, and is stunned by what it says and how negative it is. For de Niro's character, the perspective of how wonderful it is to be alive must be absent among the general population reading the newspaper.

We all want our businesses and countries to grow and flourish in these difficult times but we can only do this by bringing our workers with us, engaging them, rewarding them, nurturing them and creating livable work cultures. We could go down the line of a more ruthless management style, which micromanages people; we could focus only on the bottom line of our respective businesses or the GDP of our countries. But, as Robert Kennedy reminded us in a speech he gave on the campaign trail at the University of Kansas in 1968, shortly before his untimely and violent death in Los Angeles:

> Too much and for too long, we seemed to have surrendered personal excellence and community values in the mere accumulation of material things. Our Gross National Product, now, is over $800 billion a year, but that Gross National Product—if we judge the United States of America by that—that Gross National Product counts air pollution and cigarette advertising, and ambulances to clear our highways of carnage. It counts special locks for our doors and the jails for the people who break them. It counts the destruction of the redwood and the loss of our national wonder in chaotic sprawl. It counts napalm and counts nuclear warheads and armored cars for the police to fight the riots in our cities. It counts Whitman's rifle and Speck's knife, and the television programs that glorify violence in order to sell toys to our children. Yet GDP does not allow for the health of our children, the quality of their education or the joy of their play. It does not include the beauty of our poetry or the strength of our marriages, the intelligence of our public debate or the integrity of our public officials. It measures neither our wit nor our courage, neither our wisdom nor our learning, neither our compassion nor our devotion to our country, it measures everything in short, except that which makes life worthwhile.[44]

# Notes

## Introduction and Background

1. http://www.bloomberg.com/news/2011-12-06/bloomberg-news-responds-to-bern-anke-criticism.html.
2. http://www.gpoaccess.gov/fcic/fcic.pdf, p. 354.
3. D. Bowles and C. Cooper (2009) *Employee Morale: Driving Performance in Challenging Times*. Basingstoke: Palgrave Macmillan.

## 1   The Crash of 2008: What Happened and Why Did It Happen?

1. http://www.gpoaccess.gov/fcic/fcic.pdf, p. 354.
2. Ibid.
3. Federal National Mortgage Association and Federal Home Mortgage Corporation, respectively.
4. http://en.wikipedia.org/wiki/Glass-Steagall_Act.
5. http://www.marketwatch.com/story/super-rich-ceos-are-killing-your-retirement-2011-04-05.
6. http://www.phy.bris.ac.uk/people/enderby_je/index.html.
7. http://physicsworld.com/cws/article/print/1294.
8. http://dealbreaker.com/2010/11/james-gorman-wants-every-narcissistic-wall-streeter-to-know-theyre-not-special.
9. Mr. Gorman became CEO and President of Morgan Stanley on January 1, 2010.
10. By the time he became CEO, he had only spent nine years as a Wall Street executive; he was for some time before that a consultant at McKinsey and Company.
11. T. E. Deal and A. A. Kennedy (2000) Corporate *Cultures: The Rites and Rituals of Corporate Life*, Revised edition. Cambridge, MA:Da Capo Press, p. 4.
12. M. Bower (1966) *The Will to Manage.*New York: McGraw Hill (original source of Deal and Kennedy quote given earlier).
13. http://www.sec.gov/news/press/2010/2010-123.htm.
14. Ibid.
15. http://motherjones.com/politics/2010/01/joseph-stiglitz-wall-street-morals.
16. http://www.rollingstone.com/politics/news/why-isnt-wall-street-in-jail-20110216?page=1.
17. http://www.freshfields.com/publications/pdfs/2010/oct10/29112.pdf.
18. http://motherjones.com/politics/2010/01/financial-crisis-wall-street-anger.
19. http://online.wsj.com/article/SB10001424052748703673604575550243700895762.html.
20. Ibid.
21. http://motherjones.com/politics/2010/01/joseph-stiglitz-wall-street-morals.
22. http://en.wikipedia.org/wiki/Privatizing_profits_and_socializing_losses.
23. We are referring here to the "birthers" who have spent years demanding original copies of President Obama's Hawaiian birth certificate, believing that he is not native born and therefore not permitted to be President.

24. http://online.wsj.com/article/SB10001424052748704124504576118674203902898.html.


2   A Benefit of the Crash: More Focus on Culture and Engagement at Work

1. C. L. Cooper and S. Finkelstein (2011) *Advances in Mergers and Acquisitions*. Bingley: Emerald Publishing.
2. http://en.wikipedia.org/wiki/IBM.
3. http://www.director.co.uk/MAGAZINE/2011/2_Feb/terry-leahy_64_06.html.
4. http://doonesbury.com/strip/archive/2010/02/28.
5. D. Bowles and C. Cooper (2009) *Employee Morale: Driving Performance in Challenging Times*. Basingstoke: Palgrave Macmillan.
6. http://www.hilti.com/holcom/page/module/home/browse_main.jsf?lang=en&nodeId=-8521.
7. http://www.hilti.com/holcom/page/module/home/browse_main.jsf?lang=en&nodeId=-8524.
8. http://www.macstories.net/roundups/inspirational-steve-jobs-quotes/.
9. http://www.wired.com/magazine/2011/03/mf_larrypage/all/1.
10. http://googlesystem.blogspot.com/2005/10/google-corporate-values.html.
11. http://davidbowles.wordpress.com/2010/07/09/shrm-2010-conference-the-blog-outtakes-2-vineet-nayar-and-googles-shannon-deegan/.
12. http://www.amazon.com/Employees-First-Customers-Second-Conventional/dp/1422139069/ref=sr_1_1?s=books&ie=UTF8&qid=1303321095&sr=1-1.
13. D. Macleod and C. Brady (2008) *The Extra Mile: How to Engage to Win*. London: Prentice Hall.
14. http://commguide.asu.edu/brand/values.
15. Buffett is known as the "Oracle of Omaha," the Nebraska city where he lives and works.
16. http://dealbook.nytimes.com/2011/05/02/warren-buffett-lets-the-facts-bury-sokol/.
17. P. Sparrow, M. Hird, A. Hesketh and C. L. Cooper (2010) *Leading HR*. London: Palgrave Macmillan.
18. http://www.bis.gov.uk/files/file52215.pdf.
19. http://www.hrmagazine.co.uk/hro/news/1018911/hr-winning-engagement-argument-macleod-warns-hr-seminar.
20. D. Bowles and C. Cooper (2009) *Employee Morale: Driving Performance in Challenging Times*. Basingstoke: Palgrave Macmillan.
21. They usually do this with the help of surveys, which we have detailed in *Employee Morale*, such as Gallup's well-known Q-12. Finding out how workers feel about the organization without such a tool, while generating valid data, is almost impossible, as we have discussed at length in that book.
22. I. Robertson and C. L. Cooper (2011) *Wellbeing: Productivity and Happiness at Work*. London: Palgrave Macmillan.
23. D. Bowles and C. Cooper (2009) *Employee Morale: Driving Performance in Challenging Times*. Basingstoke: Palgrave Macmillan; see Chapter 3.
24. http://www.bis.gov.uk/files/file52215.pdf.
25. http://en.wikipedia.org/wiki/Lost_Decade_%28Japan%29.
26. http://www.kenexa.com/MediaRoom/PressReleases/2010/Kenexa-Research-Institute-Announces-Publication-of.

27. http://english.peopledaily.com.cn/90001/90776/90883/6865765.html.
28. The UK is excluded here because it had privatized most state-owned companies long before the large continental telecoms and others were obliged to do so.
29. http://en.wikipedia.org/wiki/France_T%C3%A9l%C3%A9com.
30. http://www.ft.com/cms/s/0/6cf3f994-4437-11df-b327-00144feab49a.html#axzz1G8a4jL86.
31. France Télécom's workers were civil servants during this time and by all accounts FT has not had mass layoffs of such workers, perhaps for this reason, instead cutting staff levels by attrition only or offering buyouts.
32. *NBC Nightly News*, March 4, 2011; "America at a Crossroads" segment on women in the workplace.
33. http://www4.gsb.columbia.edu/ideasatwork/feature/137194/When+women+rank+high,+firms+profit.
34. *NBC Nightly News*, see #32.
35. C. Gatrell, C. L. Cooper and E. Kossek (2010) *Women and Management*, Volumes 1 and 2. Cheltenham: Edward Elgar Publishing.
36. We use the phrase "national culture" to differentiate it from the "organizational" or "corporate" culture, which is a large part of the focus of this book.
37. Until 2010, Germany was the world's largest exporter, but this rank has been overtaken now by China.
38. http://gmj.gallup.com/content/117376/employee-disengagement-plagues-germany.aspx#1
39. ibid.
40. Advocacy relates to whether the worker would recommend their current employer as a place to work to others, or as a place with which to do business, etc.
41. Gallup reiterates our previous example of this formality by mentioning that people who have worked sometimes decades together often still use the formal "Sie" instead of the informal "Du" (you). This occurs even among workers at the same level.
42. http://gmj.gallup.com/content/117376/employee-disengagement-plagues-germany.aspx#1
43. http://davidbowles.wordpress.com/2010/11/13/why-is-european-customer-service-so-bad/.
44. http://www.bis.gov.uk/assets/biscore/corporate/migratedd/publications/g/gateways_to_the_professions_report.pdf, p. 20.
45. S. Cartwright and C. L. Cooper (2008) *Oxford Handbook of Personnel Psychology*. Oxford: Oxford University Press.
46. The Minnesota Multiphasic Personality Inventory; this is usually administered and interpreted by a professional psychologist due to its complexity.
47. http://www.haygroup.com/EngagementMatters/press/uk.aspx.
48. Ibid.
49. This is why many organizations use much broader-based questionnaire tools. For an example, see C. L. Cooper, S. Cartwright and B. Faragher (2004) *ASSET: An Organizational Stress Screening Tool*. Manchester: RCL.
50. J. K. Harter, F. L. Schmidt and T. L. Hayes (2002) "Business-Unit-Level Relationship between Employee Satisfaction, Employee Engagement, and Business Outcomes: A Meta-analysis," *Journal of Applied Psychology*, Vol. 87, No. 2, pp. 268–79.
51. D. Bowles and C. Cooper (2009) *Employee Morale: Driving Performance in Challenging Times*. Basingstoke: Palgrave Macmillan, p. 168 (original Mercer data not available online).

52. http://davidbowles.wordpress.com/2010/03/02/employee-satisfaction-down-but-engagement-flat-how-can-that-be/.
53. D. Bowles and C. Cooper (2009) *Employee Morale: Driving Performance in Challenging Times*. Basingstoke: Palgrave Macmillan, p. 188.
54. http://www.worldatwork.org/waw/adimLink?id=34569.
55. http://www.thefreelibrary.com/Despite+the+Downturn%2c+Employees+Remain+Engaged%3b+But+there+are...-a0217073117.
56. http://uk.mercer.com/rewardsurvey.
57. http://www.haygroup.com/EngagementMatters/press/uk.aspx.
58. Ibid.
59. http://gmj.gallup.com/content/117376/employee-disengagement-plagues-germany.aspx.
60. http://www.kenexa.com/MediaRoom/PressReleases/2010/Kenexa-Research-Institute-Announces-Publication-of.
61. http://www.towerswatson.com/global-workforce-study/reports.
62. Ibid.
63. Ibid.
64. http://www.towerswatson.com/assets/pdf/1455/GWS-UK-exec-sum.pdf.
65. http://www.shrm.org/Publications/hrmagazine/EditorialContent/2010/1210/trend-book/Pages/default.aspx.
66. Specific engagement percentages in the US (28–31%) and Germany (13%) for particular time periods can be directly compared with each other because they are both generated using the same (Gallup) methodology.

## 3   Ego at Work: The Common Thread between the Crash and Low Engagement

1. A credible example of this is in the writings of Eckhart Tolle, such as *The Power of Now* and *A New Earth*. Tolle was suicidal in his late 20s, and at the depth of his despair he experienced a sudden and major spiritual breakthrough; after this he wrote that he had been freed from an ego-based life. *A New Earth* is a treasure trove of his writing on the ego, with no less than 100 of its 300+ pages dedicated to that subject, probably better and more understandable for nonpsychologists (and even for those of us in that profession) than that found in any psychologically based publications. Tolle fully understands and explains the canny nature of the ego, its various disguises, and the widespread havoc it wreaks.
2. http://dictionary.reference.com/browse/ego.
3. http://wordnetweb.princeton.edu/perl/webwn?s=ego&sub=Search+WordNet&o2=&o0=1&o7=&o5=&o1=1&o6=&o4=&o3=&h=.
4. Ego's ability to feed on separation is demonstrated by its fondness for making others as bad as possible in relation to ourselves, even to the point of them being "enemies." It justifies this with all kinds of rationale, but the process remains the same: "me" versus "you," or separation.
5. *Persona* comes from the Latin for "mask," a very appropriate word in this context.
6. J. M. Twenge and W. K. Campbell (2009) *The Narcissism Epidemic: Living in the Age of Entitlement*. New York: Free Press.
7. http://www.great-quotes.com/quotes/author/Mahatma/Gandhi.
8. The origin of this is unknown, but we are grateful for it, whoever it was.
9. *The Narcissism Epidemic*, see note 6.

10. http://www.narcissismepidemic.com/.

11. *The Narcissism Epidemic*, see note 6, p. 2

12. *The Narcissism Epidemic*, see note 6, p. 127.

13. http://en.wikipedia.org/wiki/Barings_Bank.

14. http://www.nytimes.com/2010/10/06/business/global/06bank.html.

15. http://online.wsj.com/article/SB10001424052748704124504576118421859347048.html.

16. http://bottomline.msnbc.msn.com/_news/2011/11/28/9069505-wall-street-pay-bonuses-to-plummet-this-year.

17. Data Source 1: http://blogs.hbr.org/hbr/how-to-fix-executive-pay/2009/06/why-high-ceo-pay-is-bad-business.html.

18. Data Source 2: http://www.faireconomy.org/files/executive_excess_2008.pdf.

19. Data Source 3: http://www.graefcrystal.com/images/ceo_worker_pay_ratios_web_7_1_08.pdf.

20. *Fortune* magazine, November 7, 2011, p. 28.

21. http://www.graefcrystal.com/images/ceo_worker_pay_ratios_web_7_1_08.pdf.

22. http://philebersole.wordpress.com/2010/09/22/graef-crystal-and-the-question-of-ceo-pay/.

23. http://www.graefcrystal.com/images/ceo_worker_pay_ratios_web_7_1_08.pdf.

24. http://www2.gsu.edu/~wwwseh/Behind%20Nardelli%27s%20Abrupt%20Exit.pdf.

25. http://money.cnn.com/2005/02/12/news/newsmakers/fiorina_severance/index.htm.

26. http://www.nbcbayarea.com/news/business/NATLWagoner-Will-Walk-With-23-Million.html.

27. The underpinnings of Welch's performance have been under the microscope since his retirement: his reputation as "neutron Jack," or someone who fired many and left only the buildings, is partly to blame, as was his practice of "culling" the lowest 10% performers each year. His returns to shareholders, however, were spectacular.

28. http://en.wikipedia.org/wiki/Jack_Welch.

29. http://www.thesmokinggun.com/documents/crime/ge-brings-good-things-jack-welch.

30. http://www.businessweek.com/bwdaily/dnflash/sep2004/nf20040924_8648_db016.htm.

31. http://www.thesmokinggun.com/documents/crime/ge-brings-good-things-jack-welch.

32. http://en.wikipedia.org/wiki/Jack_Welch.

33. Estimates of Welch's net worth range from the quoted amount of $720 million in 2006 to $880 million at the time of his retirement in 2001.

34. http://blogs.hbr.org/hbr/how-to-fix-executive-pay/2009/06/why-high-ceo-pay-is-bad-business.html.

35. http://financialservices.house.gov/pdf/ExecCompIPSCCPPointCounterpoint.pdf.

36. http://web.orange.co.uk/article/news/review_into_public_sector_top_bosses_salaries.

37. *The New York Times*, October 6, 2011, www.nytimes.com/2011/10/06/business/fed-sees-progress-in-bank-compensation-plans.html.

38. http://www.prescott.edu/faculty_staff/faculty/scorey/documents/drucker_1998.pdf.

39. *New Perspectives Quarterly*,Vol. 15, No. 2, pp. 4–12, Spring 1998, as quoted in http://www.prescott.edu/faculty_staff/faculty/scorey/documents/drucker_1998.pdf.

40. http://archives.citypaper.net/articles/2009/06/18/fair-pay-for-fat-cats.

41. http://en.wikipedia.org/wiki/Economic_inequality.

42. http://archives.citypaper.net/articles/2009/06/18/fair-pay-for-fat-cats.

43. *The New York Times*, October 6, 2011. http://www.nytimes.com/2011/10/06/business/a-manifesto-for-wall-street-protesters.html.
44. C. L. Cooper and S. Finkelstein (2011) *Advances in Mergers and Acquisitions*. Bingley: Emerald Publishing.
45. http://knowledge.wharton.upenn.edu/article.cfm?articleid=1137.
46. Ibid.
47. http://www.nytimes.com/2010/05/30/fashion/30FACEBOOK.html?pagewanted=all.
48. http://jobs.aol.com/articles/2011/03/31/why-your-manager-doesnt-like-you-and-what-you-can-do-about-it/?icid=main%7Chtmlws-main-n%7Cdl11%7Csec1_lnk1%7C208399.
49. D. Bowles and C. Cooper (2009) *Employee Morale: Driving Performance in Challenging Times*. Basingstoke: Palgrave Macmillan; see Chapters 3 and 4.
50. *The American Heritage® Stedman's Medical Dictionary*. Retrieved on April 5, 2011, from Dictionary.com: http://dictionary.reference.com/browse/organization.
51. E. Tolle (2006) *A New Earth: Awakening to Your Life's Purpose*. New York: Plume, a member of Penguin (USA), p. 123.
52. D. Cowherd and D. Levine (1992) "Product Quality and Pay Equity," *Administrative Science Quarterly*, 37, June, pp. 302–330, quoted in http://www.huppi.com/kangaroo/L-richmerit.htm.
53. Quoted in J. Byrne (1996) "How High Can CEO Pay Go?" *Business Week*, April 22.
54. http://www.wiwi.uni-hannover.de/Forschung/Diskussionspapiere/dp-435.pdf.
55. J. S. Adams (1965) "Inequity in Social Exchange." In L. Berkowitz (ed.) *Advances in Experimental Social Psychology*, Vol. 2, pp. 267–299, New York: Academic Press.
56. Ibid.

## 4　Balancing Me and We: Building a Sustainable, High Engagement Work Culture

1. http://www.cbsnews.com/stories/2003/07/03/60minutes/main561656.shtml.
2. http://en.wikipedia.org/wiki/Malden_Mills.
3. Of course, mankind has a long history of ignoring certain of these principles of balance outside the organizational realm as well. Some believe, for example, that human-driven climate change/global warming is one of the outcomes of this. The world's exploding human population is also an issue of balance, as any species in the same situation over the eons has discovered.
4. I. Robertson and C. L. Cooper (2011). *Wellbeing: Productivity and Happiness at Work*. London: Palgrave Macmillan.
5. See also C. L. Cooper and S. Wood (2011) "The Happiness Business", *The Guardian*, London, July 16 (www.guardian.co.uk).
6. We will discuss cognitive intelligence (IQ) and emotional intelligence (EQ) later in this chapter.
7. We are aware of the argument that factors such as profitability and positive customer feedback can also raise worker morale and therefore, engagement. However, our own research and that of others, extensively presented in *Employee Morale*, demonstrated that the main direction of cause and effect is worker → customer and not the other way around. Other research has also shown this for financial performance factors.
8. Wikipedia reports that Boesky had given a speech on greed at the University of California, Berkeley in 1986.
9. http://en.wikipedia.org/wiki/Gordon_Gekko.

10. V. F. Asaro, J.D. (2011) *Universal Co-opetition: Nature's Fusion of Cooperation and Competition*, San Diego, CA: Bettie Youngs Books (www.bettieyoungs.com).

11. http://www.amazon.com/s/ref=nb_sb_ss_c_1_11?url=search-alias%3Dstripbooks& field-keywords=co-opetition&sprefix=co-opetition.

12. See *I Am* (2011 release), a film by successful Hollywood director and producer Tom Shadyac who delves into this and other related subjects (www.iamthedoc.com).

13. http://news.softpedia.com/news/Why-Do-Birds-Fly-in-V-Formation-52785.shtml.

14. http://en.wikiquote.org/wiki/Steve_Jobs.

15. http://en.wikipedia.org/wiki/History_of_Apple_Inc.#1985-1997:_Sculley.2C_Spindler.2C_Amelio.

16. http://en.wikipedia.org/wiki/Apple_Computer,_Inc._v._Microsoft_Corporation.

17. http://en.wikipedia.org/wiki/History_of_Apple_Inc.#1985-1997:_Sculley.2C_Spindler.2C_Amelio.

18. Sadly, Apple co-founder and CEO Steve Jobs died while we were finishing the writing for this book. He will be sorely missed, and remembered as one of the greatest entrepreneurial geniuses of all time.

19. http://www.slate.com/id/2267342/entry/2267344.

20. Ibid.

21. http://www.imdb.com/title/tt0140447/usercomments.

22. We are grateful to San Diego-based life scientist Dr. Victor Manneh of Xen Biosciences for this example.

23. http://psychcentral.com/news/2006/09/12/nicotine-as-an-antidepressant/258.html.

24. http://atlasshrugged.com/2010/05/atlas-shrugged-selling-in-record-numbers/.

25. http://seattletimes.nwsource.com/html/opinion/2011971537_will28.html.

26. "Man—every man—is an end in himself, not a means to the ends of others; he must live for his own sake, neither sacrificing himself to others nor sacrificing others to himself; he must work for his rational self-interest, with the achievement of his own happiness as the highest moral purpose of his life." From Ayn Rand Institute (www.aynrand.org): *The Essentials of Objectivism*.

27. Balance is organization and industry specific; like culture, one size does not fit all. But some aspects *such as balancing "me" and "we"* are universal.

28. P. F. Drucker (2008) *Managing Oneself*, reprint. Boston, MA: Harvard Business Press. http://www.google.com/search?tbo=p&tbm=bks&q=bibliogroup:%22Harvard+Business+review+classics%22&source=gbs_metadata_r&cad=8

29. This is the affectionate name given by students to a long-running program at Stanford, one of many that they have in this area.

30. http://online.wsj.com/article/SB10001424052748704740604576301491797067346.html.

31. Ibid.

32. http://www.businessweek.com/bschools/content/aug2007/bs2007082_280172.htm.

33. http://books.google.com/books?id=AcJ7dwsnWiIC&dq=emotional+intelligence&hl=en&ei=VQLUTdKmGtLSiALS4YiyBA&sa=X&oi=book_result&ct=result&resnum=1&ved=0CDsQ6AEwAA.

34. http://www.amazon.com/Primal-Leadership-Learning-Emotional-Intelligence/dp/1591391849/ref=sr_1_7?ie=UTF8&qid=1305740144&sr=8-7.

35. http://online.wsj.com/article/SB10001424052748704740604576301181974037002.html.

36. Statement in The *Computerworld* Smithsonian Awards Program oral history, April 20 1995, quoted in http://en.wikiquote.org/wiki/Steve_Jobs.

37. http://www.bis.gov.uk/files/file52215.pdf.
38. You do not have to use the word "values." You can say: "Organizations place a lot of importance for day-to-day work life on different things: which of the following do you believe are important to [your organization's name]?"
39. http://www.shrm.org/Publications/hrmagazine/EditorialContent/Pages/0209grossman.aspx.
40. http://www.shrm.org/Publications/hrmagazine/EditorialContent/Pages/0209grossman1.aspx.
41. Ibid.
42. http://www.apa.org/releases/telecommuting.html.
43. J. W. Wiley and S. M. Brooks (2000) "The High Performance Organizational Climate."In N. M. Ashkanasy, C. Wilderom and M. F. Peterson (eds) *Handbook of Organizational Culture and Climate*. Thousand Oaks, CA: Sage, p. 183.
44. http://davidbowles.wordpress.com/2010/03/08/troubling-issue-in-consultants-employee-engagement-trend-data-why-do-they-differ/.
45. D. Bowles and C. Cooper (2009) *Employee Morale: Driving Performance in Challenging Times*. Basingstoke: Palgrave Macmillan; see Chapter 4.
46. http://en.wikipedia.org/wiki/Enron.
47. http://www.amazon.com/Servant-Leader-Creative-Bottom-Line-Performance/dp/1400054737.
48. http://www.leadersdirect.com/critique-of-servant-leadership.
49. We are not denying that an occasional and unscrupulous manager cannot find a way to "bribe" his people into scoring much higher on even a longer survey than they otherwise would. One should always be on the lookout for this: sometimes it is even mentioned by some of the "bribed" employees in the survey's own open-ended section, an ultimate irony. Any good survey can easily identify such superficial managers from the various questions that look at how workers rate them.
50. http://www.shrm.org/Publications/hrmagazine/EditorialContent/2011/0411/Pages/0411tyler.aspx. (Note: *SHRM membership may be required for access*.)
51. We recall that at one time Google had a space program!
52. http://www.economist.com/node/17035923.
53. http://www.scribd.com/doc/46420008/Informed-Employee-Voice-and-Organizational-Engagement.
54. http://davidbowles.wordpress.com/2011/02/04/twitter-and-facebook-are-agents-of-engagement-at-work/.
55. http://www.safetynewsalert.com/bp-well-blowout-investigation-safety-lessons-for-all/#more-9301.
56. Men are also increasingly being given time off by organizations during and after the time of childbirth, etc.
57. http://career-advice.monster.com/job-search/company-industry-research/women-friendly-employers/article.aspx.
58. http://davidbowles.wordpress.com/2011/03/18/women-as-leaders-good-for-worker-engagement-and-organization-performance/.
59. http://www.apa.org/releases/telecommuting.html.
60. http://www.efesonline.org/Annual%20Economic%20Survey/2010/Presentation.htm.
61. http://money.cnn.com/2010/07/06/news/companies/employee_stock_options/index.htm.
62. http://www.bis.gov.uk/files/file52215.pdf, p. 113.
63. We used the word "hungry" advisedly because of the high unemployment in major swaths of the world economy outside of Asia at the time of writing. The number of

talented and well-qualified people out of work is a sad testament to the after-effects of the Crash and the very human costs it has generated.

64. http://www.bis.gov.uk/files/file52215.pdf, p. 115.
65. D. Bowles and C. Cooper (2009) *Employee Morale: Driving Performance in Challenging Times*. Basingstoke: Palgrave Macmillan.
66. N. Wager, G. Fieldman and T. Hussey (2003) "The Effect on Ambulatory Blood Pressure of Working under Favourably and Unfavourably Perceived Supervisors." *Occupational and Environmental Medicine*, Vol. 60, pp. 468–474.
67. http://gmj.gallup.com/content/20770/gallup-study-feeling-good-matters-in-the.aspx.
68. http://www.linkedin.com/groups/Science-Happiness-Work-Interest-Group-2814985?mostPopular=&gid=2814985.
69. J. Pryce-Jones (2010) *Happiness at Work: Maximizing Your Psychological Capital for Success*. Chichester, UK: John Wiley.
70. I. Robertson and C. L. Cooper (2011) *Wellbeing: Productivity and Happiness at Work*. London: Palgrave Macmillan.
71. http://davidbowles.wordpress.com/2011/05/30/10-things-i-want-to-hear-about-on-morale-and-engagement-at-shrm11/#comment-189.
72. J. Pryce-Jones (2010) *Happiness at Work:Maximizing Your Psychological Capital for Success*. Chichester, UK: John Wiley.
73. http://bit.ly/jGW3K5.
74. http://wp.me/pEDK3-hb.
75. D. Bowles and C. Cooper (2009) *Employee Morale: Driving Performance in Challenging Times*. Basingstoke: Palgrave Macmillan.
76. http://money.cnn.com/magazines/fortune/bestcompanies/2011/index.html.
77. http://www.hrcapitalist.com/2010/04/what-engagement-looks-like-via-email.html.
78. http://davidbowles.wordpress.com/2010/06/01/memo-to-the-moraleengagement-survey-haters-youre-mistaken-and-here-is-why/.
79. http://davidbowles.wordpress.com/2010/07/09/shrm-2010-conference-the-blog-out-takes-2-vineet-nayar-and-googles-shannon-deegan/.
80. Our experience with questionnaires that have as many as 100–110 items is that they can easily be completed in half an hour by most people.

## 5   Case Studies for the High Engagement Culture: BMW Group and Whole Foods Market

1. http://www.dailymotion.com/video/xe94a4_new-bmw-760-li-12-cylinder_auto.
2. Although it started life as an airplane company in 1916 (Bayerische Flugzeugwerke AG (BFW)), it was not incorporated as Bayerische Motoren Werke G. m. b. H until the next year, according to the 2010 Annual Report.
3. http://en.wikipedia.org/wiki/BMW#Company_history.
4. http://money.cnn.com/magazines/fortune/global500/2011/full_list/.
5. http://davidbowles.wordpress.com/2010/03/15/executive-excess-eroding-employee-morale-and-engagement-at-work/.
6. http://www.businessweek.com/globalbiz/content/oct2009/gb20091027_769351.htm.
7. http://www.csr-ukraine.org/bmw_group.html?lang=en.
8. https://www.press.bmwgroup.com/pressclub/p/pcgl/pressDetail.html?outputChannelId=6&id=T0100159EN&left_menu_item=node__2201.

9. BMW 2010 Annual Report, available in English (other languages also available) online at http://geschaeftsbericht.bmwgroup.com/2010/gb/files/pdf/en/BMW_Group_AR2010.pdf.

10. BMW 2010 Annual Report, p. 155, see note 8.

11. BMW 2010 Annual Report, see note 8.

12. http://www.universumglobal.com/Newsroom/News/Global-News/Europes-Ideal-Employers-2011.

13. It is worth recalling that BMW's ratio of fixed to variable, "at-risk" pay for top management, is the reverse of this at an impressive 20:80%, *if the target bonus is met* (BMW Group Annual Report, 2010, p. 155).

14. A 360 Review involves asking those directly above, at the same level and those directly below in the organizational structure to review one's performance as a manager. It is a powerful and very democratic management tool.

15. One of BMW's biggest changes for years is its move to manufacture automobiles using lightweight, strong, carbon fiber; it has invested in a factory in the US state of Washington to make the basic material for this. For more information, see http://money.cnn.com/2011/09/06/autos/carbon_fiber_bmw.fortune/index.htm.

16. http://www2.wholefoodsmarket.com/blogs/jmackey/2010/03/09/creating-the-high-trust-organization/.

17. http://finance.yahoo.com/echarts?s=%5EDJI+Interactive#symbol=^dji;range=20101101,20111207;compare=wfm;indicator=volume;charttype=area;crosshair=on;ohlcvalues=0;logscale=off;source=;.

18. http://www2.wholefoodsmarket.com/blogs/jmackey/2010/05/12/keeping-our-executive-team-together-for-10-more-years/.

19. http://www.wholefoodsmarket.com/values/corevalues.php.

20. Austin is both the capital city of the state of Texas and a university town, home to the University of Texas' main campus and a football stadium for the University's football team, which rivals or surpasses that of many national teams. It has a seating capacity of more than 100,000. Austin's reputation as a somewhat "weird" piece of a very conservative state plays into Whole Foods' beginnings as a counterculture icon.

21. Whole Foods began life as "Safer Way."

22. http://www2.wholefoodsmarket.com/blogs/jmackey/2010/03/09/creating-the-high-trust-organization/.

23. http://reason.tv/video/show/john-mackey-full-interview.

24. Some of these payments might be quite high in an absolute sense, but *relative* to the extraordinary costs of most medical services in the US, they are usually quite small.

25. Recipients must pay tax if they spend these funds on a nonmedical expense, plus a 10% fee.

26. http://www.margaretthatcher.org/document/102953.

27. Whole Foods (WF) locates its stores in areas where large numbers of college graduates live, and where they can reach that store within 16 minutes. Of WF customers, 80% are college graduates. (http://reason.tv/video/show/john-mackey-full-interview).

28. http://mises.org/.

29. An example of this, which we will cover in Chapter 6, is the *Occupy Wall Street* movement, which is rapidly expanding across the US as we write.

30. http://reason.tv/video/show/john-mackey-full-interview.

31. http://www2.wholefoodsmarket.com/blogs/jmackey/category/conscious-capitalism/.

32. www2.wholefoodsmarket.com/blogs/jmackey/2011/06/24/defending-morality-capitalism/.

33. http://blogs.hbr.org/hbr/how-to-fix-executive-pay/2009/06/why-high-ceo-pay-is-bad-business.html.
34. http://www.davispolk.com/briefing/corporategovernance/?entry=106.
35. http://www2.wholefoodsmarket.com/blogs/jmackey/2010/03/09/creating-the-high-trust-organization/.
36. http://www.wholefoodsmarket.com/meat/welfare.php.
37. This might be seen as far more likely to be the case for Whole Foods' "high end," college-educated customer base, but we also note that even Walmart has become a major retailer of organic food, indicating that these values are far from socioeconomically limited.
38. http://reason.tv/video/show/john-mackey-full-interview.
39. Ibid.
40. Ibid.
41. Ibid.

## 6   Why All This Matters So Much, and Where We Go From Here

1. The *Arab Spring* has become the *Arab Autumnand Winter* and intensified with the death of Muammar Gaddafi on October 20, 2011 and what appears to be a move toward civil war in Syria.
2. http://blogs.wsj.com/wealth/2010/04/30/top-1-increased-their-share-of-wealth-in-financial-crisis/.
3. http://www.nytimes.com/2011/10/26/us/politics/top-earners-doubled-share-of-nations-income-cbo-says.html?_r=1.
4. http://en.wikipedia.org/wiki/United_States_presidential_approval_rating.
5. http://www.realclearpolitics.com/epolls/2012/president/president_obama_vs_republican_candidates.html.
6. http://www.opensecrets.org/lobby/incdec.php.
7. Poll reported on *Hardball with Chris Matthews*, MSNBC, October 26, 2011.
8. http://www.indexmundi.com/g/g.aspx?v=66&c=ch&l=en.
9. http://www.whatsonsanya.com/news-15470-china-s-2011-economic-growth-rate-to-hit-9-world-bank.html.
10. http://online.wsj.com/article/SB10001424052748704104104575622531909154228.html.
11. Ibid.
12. http://www.nytimes.com/2006/11/26/business/yourmoney/26every.html
13. In 2010 Buffett had total income of over $60 million, net income (after deductions such as charitable contributions) of $40 million, and paid some $7 million, or 17%, in tax. See reference #14.
14. http://www.washingtonpost.com/blogs/plum-line/post/yup-the-buffett-and-his-secretary-analogy-is-completely-accurate/2011/10/13/gIQAj3NYhL_blog.html.
15. http://www.celebritynetworth.com/articles/entertainment-articles/how-much-money-warren-buffett-make-2010/.
16. http://www.huffingtonpost.com/2010/10/05/warren-buffett-tax-cuts_n_751503.html.
17. We are grateful to V. Frank Asaro, J.D. for this observation.
18. http://hbr.org/2011/01/the-big-idea-creating-shared-value/ar/1.
19. Ibid.
20. Ibid.

21. Ibid.
22. Ibid.
23. Ibid.
24. Ibid.
25. D. Bowles and C. Cooper (2009) *Employee Morale: Driving Performance in Challenging Times*. Basingstoke: Palgrave Macmillan.
26. For more on morale and engagement as "touchy-feely" go to: http://wp.me/pEDK3-dU.
27. http://www.shrm.org/Publications/hrmagazine/EditorialContent/2011/0811/Pages/0811cappelli.aspx.
28. P. Cappelli, H. Singh, J. Singh and M. Useem (2010) *The India Way: How India's Top Business Leaders are Revolutionizing Management*.Boston: Harvard Business Press.
29. Ibid.
30. Cappelli uses Vineet Nayar (previously mentioned here), CEO of India-based HCL Technologies as his example of this very comprehensive approach to engagement, which is detailed in Nayar's book *Employees First, Customers Second* (2010), Boston: Harvard Business Press Books.
31. http://online.wsj.com/article/SB10001424052970204422404576596630897409182.html?mod=WSJ_hp_mostpop_read.
32. His observation refers to the US but is relevant for any country that looks to the US for the best management ideas. In this case, the US needs to look elsewhere itself.
33. http://hbr.org/2011/01/the-big-idea-creating-shared-value/ar/1.
34. http://www.americanprogress.org/issues/2009/05/millennial_generation.html.
35. The seven billionth person arrived here, according to the UN, as we were writing this last chapter.
36. http://www.guardian.co.uk/environment/interactive/2011/oct/28/world-population-growth-7-billionth-person?INTCMP=SRCH.
37. For just one example, we look at the terrible pollution that communism left behind. For an ideology supposedly "of the people" it had nothing but contempt for the environment in which those people lived—and died.
38. http://sanfrancisco.ibtimes.com/articles/153551/20110527/north-korea-happiness-index-rank-china-top-us-bottom-photos.htm.
39. http://en.wikipedia.org/wiki/Happy_Planet_Index.
40. http://sq.4mg.com/NationHappiness.htm.
41. http://www.iim-edu.org/grossnationalhappiness/.
42. Ibid.
43. http://en.wikipedia.org/wiki/Gross_national_happiness.
44. http://www.jfklibrary.org/Research/Ready-Reference/RFK-Speeches/Remarks-of-Robert-F-Kennedy-at-the-University-of-Kansas-March-18-1968.aspx.

# Index